The Importance of Discipline

E.L Discipline

Andrea Johnson Books Publishing

"If you don't believe in anything, you should believe in Discipline
– E.L Discipline

The Importance of Discipline

Cover art designed by Andrea Johnson Books Publishing.

First published by Andrea Johnson Books Publishing 12/19/2017

Re-released by Andrea Johnson Books Publishing 04/28/2019

6565 N. MacArthur Blvd, Suite 225 Dallas, TX. 75039
www.Ajbpublishing.com

ISBN-13: 978-0692997093

ISBN-10: 0692997091

Contents

Chapter 1 – Patience

If you can master physical and mental Discipline, you can take on anything in this world. How a man handles himself through adversity is how he thrives or crumbles. Pressure made diamonds. Diamonds are forever. Part of Discipline is self-development. How you develop yourself is how you handle situations and people. We've all heard the old cliché, "patience is a virtue." The first type is the patience needed when facing a nuisance of some kind.

A person or a set of circumstances really irritates you, and you'd love to complain about it, but you hold your tongue, knowing that such a grievance would be petty or simply compound the problem. That person at the office who is so insufferably annoying doesn't, after all, mean to pester you. And what good will it do to moan about those potholes on your street? So you quietly endure these things. Did you know you were being virtuous in doing so?

A second type of patience is called for when facing boredom. Those who fall into a rut at work or at home often experience discomfort over the uneventful routine. To those who don't struggle with boredom, it might seem absurd to suggest it can be a serious trial. But those who endure the plague of drab routine without complaint, exhibit the virtue of patience.

A third type of patience is the most serious and significant. It is the patience required when one suffers in some way, either physically or psychologically. If you're struggling with some disease or mental illness, then patience is required of you. Or if you must assist someone else who suffers, a family member or friend, then you are called upon to be patient. Whether you bear the burden of affliction directly or indirectly, your challenge is to endure that discomfort. This doesn't mean you shouldn't cry out in your distress. Scripture, in fact, advises us to do just that, so it's appropriate because the degree of discomfort in some situations warrants complaint. But this raises some important questions: What is a complaint? And which complaints are worthy?

Is It Ever Okay to Complain?

When we complain, very often we never take into account the matter, or the individual we are complaining to. At the moment of course it doesn't seem to make a difference. Our human emotions take over, and we feel the need to express whatever issues may be at the forefront of our situation. Everyone feels at that precise moment, that the one we are arguing with, has the responsibility if not obligation, to listen to our problem, and perhaps even come up with a solution to rectify it to our satisfaction. So therefore, there is an undeniable need to pursue and convince the other individual of our side of the story.

Whether we have truly sought the validity of our own complaint is another matter. Many people just feel the satisfaction of getting their point across, regardless.

Which complaints, then, are worthy?

A worthy complaint is one that is neither petty nor pointless. So, is patience just about delaying immediate gratification? Simply put —yes. It's a lot more than just that, of course, but it makes for a good start.

It's ok to raise objections about conditions that are clearly unjust or impractical and need to be changed. But it is never necessary to worry over something you have no control over. And arguing regarding issues that are neither important nor substantial, doesn't qualify as a legitimate protest.

In today's society, you have those individuals that gain more satisfaction from simply believing they are right. The feeling of going to great lengths to illustrate their point of view is an example of this. Common sense is never a factor when this is the case. It could be something as small as not having the right amount of water poured into your glass at a restaurant. In a situation like this, it is neither relevant, nor valid to complain and pursue an argument over a waiter's inability to measure the proper amount of water. It is apparently just the pleasure of making the individual aware that you are displeased. And that is never a good enough reason to complain about anything.

A worthy complaint should represent the basis between right and wrong. A clear indication in a situation where the complainer has a logical and factual evidence as to why they are arguing their point. You can look at it as if you were in a court of law. You are considered innocent, until proven guilty. If you cannot prove someone's guilt, with credible evidence to back it up, then the accused is often set free. Having the patience to discern whether or not a complaint is worthy, is paramount to being a level headed individual.

From a health perspective, impatience contributes to stress, high blood pressure, and premature aging, among other adverse effects. From a psychological standpoint, impatience leads to unnecessary risks and poor decisions. From a social point of view, being impatient is a guaranteed way of losing friends and making enemies. It's also just not very attractive. And since you're no longer a pre-schooler, the stakes are now much higher than losing an extra marshmallow!

While there are certain situations that can affect your patience, like medication, and eating certain foods too late in the evening, there are many ways you can achieve a more balanced outlook. A path to becoming a calmer, happier, more patient presence within oneself, in relationships, in the workplace, and in the world. The development of genuine, open-minded patience may very well lead one to also examine one's experience of anger and its root causes.

The path that develops patience is travelled along a journey similar to that which undermines the deceiving appeal of anger, and what at times can appear to be anger's uncontrollable nature. Although impatience and anger are not the same, they live in the same neighbourhood. In fact, it is as if they live in the same place with hardly anything between them, anger ready to join in when impatience shows the slightest interest in emerging from its thin-shelled cocoon.

Anger is something else entirely. It is the exact opposite of patience, yet not exactly mirroring impatience. Anger is a full-blown emotion that simply controls all aspects of feeling at the moment. There is no reason or common sense to anything when anger is involved. Impatience is the neighbouring emotion to anger. It is often the catalyst that opens the way to anger's dominance. It is important that patience is used to alleviate the presence of anger. Because it is too easy to open yourself to loss of control, and this is why you must be diligent in keeping the two separate.

Not being emotionally and mentally shredded by the vicissitudes of life—the roller coaster ride of pleasure and pain, gain and loss, praise and blame, fame and obscurity—often requires a substantial depth of patience if one is to experience a sense of balance and joy in this precious life. The development of patience requires an understanding of the root causes of our stress, anxiety, and frustration. Then we must be willing to relinquish the type of thinking that leads to the loss of patience.

Because anger and patience are opposites, they can be thought of as two sides of the same coin. When one side is visible the other is hard to see. When patience is active, anger is unlikely to emerge. That does not mean that the patient person does not experience anger, or that the person easily disposed toward anger never displays great patience. Yes, even the most spiritual individual remains human and continues to experience human thoughts, feelings, and sensations. Even so, the progression and continuing practice of patience can be achieved, so that one does not respond in conditioned ways or with emotional reactions that can cause suffering to oneself and others.

Emotions are fragile things. They can be swayed based on induvial thought and actions. Careful consideration must be used when displaying your feelings in a matter that may cause a negative outcome of any kind. This is where patience comes in. It gives us the ability to analyse our thought process deeper. It controls our need to act without reason or logic.

Because of anger's enormous potential for danger, it is often the reason we call on patience to come to the rescue, to save the day, perhaps even to save a life. As you continue on in this book, you will explore various aspects of everyday living that can challenge the patience of the most well intentioned among us. There is never a need to wonder if you will ever know for sure the level of your patience and its strength. Rest assured that someone or something will show up to test how well your patience is developing. One thing that is a proven fact. It takes patience to develop patience, if that makes sense to you. Patience does not come easily. It is a slowly processed emotion that must grow in strength over time. It is important to understand that this will not happen overnight. Just as you would train your body and muscles to increase in stamina by constantly going to the gym, you must work on teaching your emotions to reflect patience as the primary feeling. As you continue to adapt to a more calmer approach, keep in mind, you are still human. You will have days where your patience will be sorely lacking. And it will take great strength and discipline to control the urges you are familiar with. But it will become easier in time.

Patience in corporate America

It is not often that professionals or businessmen are found with the ability of being in politics, many don't comprehend the process, they are very short tempered, and do not understand exactly what it takes to make it work. Democracy isn't a business. Being individuals, and even our preferences molds us into who we choose to be today. Many people cannot grasp that. The real decision is to choose to challenge ourselves, to investigate the inner workings of our own mind and create an atmosphere of understanding. To accept and have more tolerance, and patience. To give back even more than we try to take.

What does tolerance mean?

Tolerance is another form of patience. It is the consequence of humanity. We are all formed of frailty and error; let us pardon reciprocally each other's folly - that is the first law of nature.

To have tolerance you must learn endurance. To be able to adapt to any situation, and adjust. It is the key in learning patience and becoming a more evolved individual.

The goal here is a change of mindset. To be able to comprehend the difference between tolerance and patience, is to understand that they are elements of each other, and go hand in hand with a calm and more focused point of view. An example of tolerance is being able to put up with a situation that you know may not be a favorable one. Patience will be present here, to allow you to see it through. However, tolerance will give you the ability to endure. Tolerance and patience together allow the mind to view and operate differently. In a more logical and balanced position.

There are several ways you can incorporate patience.

Reframe the situation. Feeling impatient is sometimes assumed to be an automatic emotional response; it involves conscious thoughts and beliefs, too. If someone happens to fall through, or is late for an event, you can fume about their lack of respect, or use that extra time to do something productive. Patience is very much like self-control, and has the ability to regulate our emotions. It can help us train our self-control muscles, and change our mindset to a more level-headed approach.

Practice mindfulness. There have been studies that have shown kids who trained in patience for six months or more, to exhibit a mindfulness in more tolerance. This is just an example of how training the way you think can effect your emotions and actions.

Practice gratitude. Practicing gratitude is another study in patience. Remembering to be thankful for something, or even displaying gratefulness, can be very difficult sometimes. Especially if you do not feel very friendly towards the individual, or have a grudge against the person for some matter of other. Having gratitude, and taking the time to display even a small amount of appreciation, can go a long way in helping you to have more patience.

Why impatience is dangerous

When we get immediate gratification and convenience in our life, then we expect other areas of our life to work just as simply. But, this way of thinking causes problems when something doesn't happen as we intend it to be. It also is dangerous when we don't address an issue because it seems too difficult or appears too long to complete.

If anything ever occurs that seems too impossible for you to handle, the first natural instinct is to abandon that task, or give in to anger. The emotions tend to become cluttered with self-doubt, low self-esteem and rage. And it hinders our ability to work through our disorders without resorting to impatience.

For example, let's say you are waiting in line at a department store. The line is very long, and you've been standing there for some time. All of a sudden, the cashier in the front handling all the orders, begins to chat away with her current customer. Not caring that she has an extensive amount of people waiting on her. This of course would instil a great deal of impatience, even leading to the urge to force the situation into your favour, by emotionally releasing your anger onto the focus of your displeasure.

Also, if a task appears to be too difficult or long to finish, then we usually choose not to do it because of our desire for instant results. So we regularly settle for the shorter and more convenient path.

For example, many people don't consider careers that require grad school because they don't want to go through the extra years of schooling. I'm confident that thousands of people who would be excellent doctors, lawyers, dentists, and other professions miss out on a fulfilling and satisfying career because of a short-term mindset against more education. It's disappointing.

For another example, many people say they want to be rich. But, they're unwilling to take the necessary steps to obtain wealth, because they aren't patient. These same people say investing in the stock market "takes too long." They would rather spend their money shopping to feel the immediate happiness of buying something new (which goes away pretty soon after the purchase). Or their impatience gives them over to the get-rich-quick schemes that never work. There's a better solution to success in life, and it's called being patient.

How to become more tolerant

People will always be judged based on their ability to endure and handle various circumstances. Your capability to cope with a difficult task is what measures your tolerance level. The more tolerance you have, the less anger will be present in your emotions. Anger is the emotion of intolerance. Intolerance means that you don't accept other people's opinion or behaviour. Anger is an expression that what you think is right and the others are wrong. In short, anger could drive people to have less tolerance to others. These are three important traits of tolerant people.

- **Respect**: Being respectful is not only a key factor to being tolerant, it is paramount in leading a healthy life. When you are respectful of others, you will also respect yourself and understand the boundaries that follows this trait.

- **Peacefulness**: Intolerance causes conflicts and, in many cases, it even triggered wars. Peace is a good breeding ground to nurture tolerance. A tolerant individual never starts a conflict unnecessarily.

- **Courage**: Courage is not the absence of fear. It is the presence of tolerance and patience. It is the ability to take any given situation and view it objectively, while still being willing to pursue the challenge it reveals.

First, there are certain things you should remember. You are human. You have emotions that live and are directly impacted with everything you do or see and hear. You must learn to control these emotions, so that you do not become addicted to the urge or impulse reactions that often drive our inner natures to perform actions we may regret later. Putting this all in perspective can help you understand that certain things that are out of your control, are not worth getting angry over. And the things that are, can be handled efficiently, if you apply tolerance.

Further, if you want to be defensive, never act offensively (that's what intolerance is all about!), however you can do that in a wiser way by saying "Tell me more about that. I'd like to know why you come up with that opinion. This is your chance to share your thought with me.

Avoid using profanity at all costs. This often is the bridge that gives way to the rage held at bay within all of us. It's very easy to express and often the best way to display our impatience with someone. But regardless of the need, there are other ways to communicate without doing this.

Look for points of agreement. Nowadays, free sex is one of parent's problems. However, when parents come up with the idea by giving their daughter birth control pills for example, it is better if at the beginning of the discussion you clearly mention that you are concerned about your daughter's health and the well-being of your daughter.

Finally, you should avoid contempt. This can be displayed in many ways, through body language, verbal communication, or even a look within the eyes. Although easier said than done, contempt should be avoided, as it will only induce less tolerance and more anger to make its presence known.

A person who learns to cultivate his mind, must be able to tolerate things that he sees and feels. Having enough patience can motivate an individual to elevate to levels that will achieve greater results than animosity.

Seeking Diversity in All Things

Intolerant behaviour is oftentimes the results of being around other individuals or family members that have exhibited this kind of emotion. This is also a defining factor in how your mindset is developed over time. Who you associate with can have an impact on your attitude and outlook on things. It can directly modify your life in a positive or detrimental way. Seek to change your environment to a more focused and inspired surroundings. This may not affect things immediately, but you will begin to see results over a period of time.

Nothing can be achieved without extra effort, including understanding the idea of diversity. These are several clues to help you implement your acceptance to diversity:

-Buy newspapers from places other than where you live. If you're from a small town in the Midwest, subscribe to the New York Times. On the other hand, if you live in New York City, you can request your other relatives who live in a small town to send you her/his hometown paper.

- If you want to treat your friends, try to go to different restaurants every time you do it. This forces you out of your comfort zone.

- When you go to an event, look for the person you don't already know and start up an interesting conversation. If you only talk to the people you know, you're less likely to discover something new. Try something different.

- Travel any chance you get. As much as money allows. You can try to go to different regions of the country (or the world). When you're there, try to spend some time talking to the locals. Make a point of socializing with people from racial and ethnic backgrounds other than your own.

- Read all editorials in the newspaper every day — not just those you agree with.

- Hang around with people with different ages. You'll be amazed at how differently much younger or older folks think.

- Attend free lectures held by local and out-of-town authorities on various subjects. Most communities offer lecture series or similar cultural experiences. If you live in a very small town, look for a bigger town nearby and make a point of traveling there to take the advantage of these things.

- Remain diligent and continue to stay focused. Practice the art of listening, and observing, while doing less talking.

Avoiding Irresponsible Media

The freedom of expressing your opinion also might cause a negative result on the way you view things. Debate shows are often aired in television, and during the show an exchange opinion between "experts" are purposefully intense, loud, argumentative, and at times filled with anger. Herewith, instead of expanding your knowledge, the media foments uncivil discourse and a climate of intolerance. Leading cable news has driven and transformed the media into polarized point-counterpoint expressions at extremely contrasting viewpoints on virtually any topic you can imagine, and if you weren't angry before you started watching cable news, you will be shortly.

Without doubt, television can be entertaining and stimulating as it is a perfect blend of visual and sound. However, you need to choose which channel or media that can provide you with balanced news and is aware to their viewers. Or in other words, a media that understands about "society responsibility".

Chapter 2- Thinking

Good thoughts can never produce bad results. Bad thoughts will never produce good results. I'm a thinker. Methodical in my motives. I think before, plan ahead, think during. Think after. At the school of life, we are heavily biased towards emotional intelligence and the use of culture as a tool for consolation and enlightenment. We have some quite specific views about what makes a thinker 'great'. Typically, great thinkers are included in encyclopedia works on the basis of reputation: a list is drawn up asking what names have been most influential, and what ideas have most memorably shaped the intellectual world.

However, we've got our sights on a different aim: we want to work out what ideas offer help with some of the leading problems of our own times. For us, a 'great' thinker is someone whose ideas stand the very highest chance of being helpful in our lives now.

Because a canon is necessarily so selective, it is always vulnerable to attack. We have a sanguine view of selection; selection is simply an inescapable feature of living in an information-rich world. The ideal isn't to avoid being selective, the challenge is to try to select as well as possible. In our eyes, this means picking out thinkers who can untangle some of the greatest difficulties in our political, professional and personal lives.

We aren't historians recovering ideas for their own sakes; we are applied philosophers seeking intellectual concepts that can be put to work in the here and now. I've worked hard to make the thinkers in this book sound simple, easy and (hopefully) quite charming. In the past, many of these thinkers have been caught in a fiendish trap. What they have had to say has been hugely relevant and important. But how they have said it, has guaranteed that they went unheard: because their books were a little too dense, some of their ideas sounded odd and many of their most crucial concepts were prone to get lost amidst a welter of subsidiary information. They noticed how proud people were about being led by their instincts or passions (jumping into decisions on the basis of nothing more than 'how they felt'), and this was compared to being dragged dangerously along by a group of blindfolded wild horses. We learn to submit all our thoughts and feelings to reason. It's imperative to know thyself.

Our thought process is an integral part of our genetic makeup and design. It is what defines who you are, or who you will inevitably become. Every decision you make is what takes you closer to your aspirations and goals. But it is not simply about making the decisions. It is about how you proceed in putting together each form of action that you have created within your mind. This is a key factor in the way the mind works, in delivering the messages that your body inevitably begins to perform. It begins with the vision. I will illustrate this in more detail for you.

Having a solid vision sets the tone for positive thinking and performance. Whatever the eyes take in, the mind receives. It then communicates a message to the body within the form of the thought process, that will translate to actions that affect you in your everyday life. It is true that you are what you eat. But whatever you see or envision is what your life will be subjected to.

This is something that is very profound that most individuals do not give much credence to. It is because our society is brainwashed into believing that as long as you have money you can have or be whatever you want. This is a lie that has been used to control those of lesser knowledge, who are not educated on the true value of self-discovery. Knowing how your own mind works, and elevating what you bring to your psyche daily, goes a long way to keeping yourself and thoughts in tune with a powerful and enriching type of elevation. This goes back to having a solid vision. If you are constantly questioning yourself, why you are hesitating when making certain decisions, or feel as if you are surrounded by things that are continuously bringing down your positive energy, it is time to reevaluate what you are currently looking at.

For example. A woman can work all day and do her job efficiently, focus on every task she needs to do after work, come home and take care of her family, and still experience a drainage of her energy no matter how nice she may try to be to everyone. Her energy has become drained because of her thought process. It has absolutely nothing to do with how nice she is, or how hard she may work. If she is constantly surrounded by negative energy, and does not know how to protect her mind against it, she will become a product of her environment simply because this is what she sees and knows.

The saying has been heard many times, 'As a man thinketh, so is he' (proverbs 23:7) These words are in conjunction with the true nature of a man or woman. Whatever you think in your mind, this is what you become in actuality.

Now some may disagree and argue the point, that just because you think something bad, doesn't mean you have to do it. Generally speaking that is true. You are judged after all by your actions, not your thoughts. However, the thoughts you convey are like seeds planted within the mind. They bury deep and grow when watered over time. You may not even understand why you feel so high one day, then completely down the next. And I am not speaking about body chemistry and mood swings, either. I am referring to energy that wraps around your mind and controls the way you think and feel.

How you feel and wake up every day will eventually cause you to take action of some sort. And that is what motivates your decision and thought process. You take in what you see, you allow the seeds of negativity to be planted deep in your mind. They grow as your vision is constantly bombarded with this energy every day. Once the seeds have matured, they become thoughts. Things within your mind that form your decisions. You then suddenly choose one day you're going to quit your job, and become an actor. Regardless of the fact that you have no money, no plans, and no real blueprint of achieving that goal. Your decision was solely based on your need to compensate for the negative feelings growing in your head, which causes nothing but actions of poor thinking.

Let's take a young man within his early twenties. Currently in college, has a part time job, perhaps he's in college on half a scholarship not a full one. So he needs to pay his way through school. He's a good student, and is responsible with his job and bills. It's hard for him, but he knows that if he stays focused he can achieve his goal. Which is to graduate with a bachelors and land a good paying job. But he just so happens to have a few friends that are not in college. They have dead end jobs or are currently staying with parents and have no intention of leaving.

Every weekend this young man hangs out with these friends who are constantly going to clubs, hanging out with pretty women, and making their life appear so carefree and joyous. They encourage this man to quit school and start hustling with them, perhaps even promise him a job paying more than he would make in a year with his college degree. The young man always refuses. But a seed is planted. Each time he goes out with them, and takes part in their environment, he is subjected to the negative energy that ultimately wraps itself around his mind. This process then prompts him to one day become frustrated with his work, school, and whatever goals he was trying to obtain will seem insignificant. To the point where not even he will understand why he no longer wants what he's been working so hard to achieve. Negative energy is like a leech looking for blood. And if you do not know how to protect your mind from this, your thoughts will be subject to later on become poor actions.

So how do you protect your vision from becoming tainted by your environment? By constantly reinforcing negative energy with a positive one. Let's be realistic. Many people have to work every day in a job or place that they truly don't want to be in. But they are there because it is helping them get a little closer to the goals they are working towards. (If you are currently working at a place that in no way takes you closer to where you truly want to be, then you need to reevaluate your present occupational choices)

If you find yourself in a place that is constantly draining you, it means you are allowing seeds to enter within your mind. Counteracting this with positive solutions, helps as a vacuum to flush away these feelings that take you down. For instance, after a long day of work you soak into a bath with relaxing inspirational music. This actually sends messages to your brain waves and wipes away the shadows that plague you. Or going for a long drive and listening to your favorite music while in the car.

What you are doing is programming your thoughts, not allowing your thoughts to control you. You are creating an antidote for the mind, that will translate this healthy medicine like food is nourishment to your body.

You may not look at it that way, but that is what you are doing. Feeding your mind with positive thoughts. Your spirit will feel lighter, your body will react as if its unloaded a truck full of baggage, and your thinking will become actions that will make a positive difference in your life, and even those around you.

This is why you must protect your vision. You must be careful what you lay your eyes upon. Because humans tend to be more visually stimulated than anything else. Generally, you do not remember half of what you hear. But what you see, will be transformed into what you think and believe. And whatever you believe will later on be communicated into the decisions you will make. It is very important that you protect your thought process. Because even a small seed can one day become a plantation of crops. Be mindful of the harvest you grow in your mind.

Understanding how your mind works

The brain is a very complex yet beautiful instrument that controls the body. We use it to operate the daily functions we have come to rely on, and vastly depend on our way of life. Understanding how the mind works and transmits messages will help you comprehend how to better adapt to any environment. There are three key components that you should have knowledge of that is directly related to how the mind functions.

Frames of Mind

In this book, I have outlined three states of mind that will illustrate to you the different stages and developments within the brain. The thoughts, how we process things, and why training and fully educating yourself on this will help you to further your way of thinking.

1. Engaged Mind: We often participate in this state of mind usually when in conversation, or involved in a situation that requires personal dedication.

Being Engaged doesn't mean an absence of pain, since what might be happening at any given moment could be physically or emotionally painful. It just means being connected to whatever is going on.

For example: Some individuals may be present at a gathering and talking and listening to others, yet not completely engaged in the event taking place. It is very common to feel miles away or out of your element, yet appear to be a part or even contribute in an affair, although not be engaged in it. Full engagement requires more than just listening. You will feel connected and interested in the subject you are involved in.

2. Automatic Mind: This term primarily comes from the basis of the mind being placed on Auto-pilot. A series of actions you are performing with no thought or concern for the results of it. When in this state, you are completely detached from what you are doing, and often appear disinterested when involving others. Most individuals take on this monotone existence when faced with challenges or situations they would rather not be in. But must somehow choose to participate, regardless of their true desires.

The content of Automatic Mind is determined by current internal and environmental conditions, instincts, perceptions, and prior learning. The flow is essential for our survival and helps us adapt among countless other things, but it is also full of misinformation, distortions, and biases. We use the state of automatic mind to adapt in certain situations we are not comfortable with. It can also be used to generate feelings of automatic pleasure and joy when in a good environment. However, more often it is used to brace against the negative and undesirables. It is a form of escape.

3. Analytic Mind: We are a complex and self-aware people. Our genetic make-up allows our mind to engage and assess a pattern of things that translates into what we do and feel. How we process this information is what places this altogether, in something we can communicate and understand. This is called the Analytic mind.

In this breakdown, you will see how the analytic mind separates and dissects the different ways to process information you receive. This all correlates to the automatic mind as well. However, the analytic mind is a conscious choice you make when you turn your thought process into results.

-**Observe**: Watching other individuals, while keeping our own actions subdued.

-**Reflect**: Thinking back on previous memories that may have an effect on what you do today.

-**Solve**: To bring an immediate result to a problem that we have encountered.

-**Plan**: Carefully selecting options that will better prepare you for upcoming events.

-**Focus**: To give your attention primarily to something of importance to you.

-**Imagine**: To illustrate different outcomes in our mind, and come to a conclusion we desire.

We develop our cognitive skills early, allowing our brain to process and dissimilate information as we grow older. It really depends on the individual as well. Experiences and education will increase your analytic skills and give your brain a more in depth formation of the mind.

For example: After noticing your anxiety, you decided to try and re-Engage in the conversation. However, you stayed anxious and kept having difficulty being involved. You decided to take a couple minutes to take a closer look at your anxiety to understand why it was so strong, and to reason through it. You reflected on the earlier argument, and realized that you made a critical mistake, and you then focused on developing a plan of how to apologize and make things right again. After doing this, you are able to Engage with your friend again.

Mastering Your Mind

 Mastering your mind can be a very difficult task, but also rewarding if you apply yourself to doing it. I believe there are several important elements that will help you in learning to train and master the different frames of mind you are gifted with. It is essential that you develop your thought process to focus on positive results, regardless of what the outcome may be. This gives your way of thinking a stronger and more expansive view on success, and better living.

 Learn to be more observant and begin to process information before just utilizing it. Understand exactly how you can make a situation work to your favor, instead of against you. Focusing your mind processing information, rather than just receiving it, will change the way you perform your actions, and decisions. And this will help you to become stronger mentally, with a more developed brain, and prepared to adapt to any given situation you are faced with.

Chapter 3 – Dominance

They ask me; "How are you so clutch?" I've always been clutch, ever since I came out the womb. My mother told me when I was younger; there would be days like this. I never believed her. As I was older, the cliché, "Mothers know best", resonated. I am the cerebral assassin. The beast incarnate. The most unheralded, yet most powerful being one could ever meet. Something like that, LL Cool J track, "Phenomenon", who happens to be chocolate. Words that come out of my mouth, become reality. Thoughts. It's almost like I cast a magical spell. Vibes I send off. I am a magnetic force. The complete, and ultimate Alpha Dominant.

I thrive under pressure. I excel in any form of combat. Whether it's emotional, mental, or physical. Men are perhaps many things, but masters of nothing. DOMINANCE. What makes Dominance so relevant? Consistency. Adherence. I love Dominance. Always have. Always will. I've always been engaged in sports, and have been physically active all my life.

Winning is addictive. When I watch sports now, I see more in depth, I don't ever want to see a "good game." Most sports are rigged (however entertaining), there's no such thing as a good game. Teams are not evenly matched.

Fans want to see a good game, because they want to be entertained. They make it entertaining, because they want to give the fans their money's worth. It's like this, "let's compensate the fans." Dominance is about winning, and the reality is, most people hate seeing other people win. Not just sometimes, constantly. I want to see Dominance. No overtime. No draw. No game seven. I like to see a team get blown out. Spanked. Annihilated, destroyed. Why? Because, I know there's no evenly matched teams. That battle dancer. Martial Artist. That boxer, tennis player, wrestler, rapper, writer, author is better than his opponent or everyone else. Even mind games/sports such as chess, poker, etc. But those are the exception, because those sports require a little more work, more skill. Utilizing your most important muscle, your brain.

Sports that involve you hitting a certain target; like shooting, pool, darts, golf, bowling take more concentration. In a team sport, you must rely on others to take part in your success. You being named, "the best player in the world," is irrelevant if you don't have the best team in the world. You saying, "I am the best player in the world," on a team sport, we're not talking about one on one like boxing, but a team sport, is ridiculous. Asinine.

Dominance is the most prestigious thing in the world. Ironically, it's frowned upon? Why? Because people want to see an underdog? A Cinderella story? A happy fairy-tale ending? Fairness? That team, or he or she trains harder, and longer, wakes up earlier, strategizes better. Hard work beats talent, when talent just doesn't work hard. When you add talent and hard work, you become unstoppable. Innovative.

Discipline is the most Dominant entity you will ever witness. The disruptor of the status quo. Exception and not the rule. If these men are dogs, then it's animal cruelty. I've redefined the words, "Dominance and Discipline." A true top. Master. Dom. Alpha. Physically. Mentally, and emotionally.

So what makes Dominance and Discipline, the most prestigious aspect in life? Besides what I listed above? I appreciate those Teams like the New York Yankees in the 90's and 2000's. The New England Patriots (even though I am a Giants fan) in the 2000's. Bulls in the early 90's then late 90's. Serena Williams, Floyd Mayweather.

Circumstance does not make the man or woman; it reveals him or herself to the individual. The man or woman, as the lord and master of thought, is the maker of him or herself. The shaper and author of environment. Even at birth, the soul comes into its own, and through every step of its earthly pilgrimage, it attracts those combinations of conditions which reveal itself. Which are the reflection of its own purity and impurity, its strength and weakness. We do not get what we wish for, pray for, but what we justly earn.

As far as myself, when I'm not in control, I'm off balance and no one around me is Happy. It's a bad habit. I myself have high dominance. Directness. Assertiveness. Control. I respond to pressure with Control. I will become assertive and more aggressive expecting an immediate response to my instructions. I am motivated by achievement and control. I want to feel that I am driving the situation. I will be more respective that way. I reply better to suggestions, rather than orders. When negotiating with me use the power strategy, I will be more receptive to suggestions and hints rather than your attempts to indirectly control me, and directly control my decision making.

Men are many things, but masters of nothing. Some people are cannabis sativa, they bring you up. Provide you with a head high, inspire you, grant you with creativity, uplift you and enhance your spirit. Then there are some people whom are cannabis indica, they bring you down. Drain you. Show me the toughest man in the room. Show me the most gangster woman, then give them a paragraph to read out loud or a microphone in front of them, I want to see something real quick.

Dominance will never die. And Sexy will constantly be intriguing. All three have ties. Because, you can obtain whatever you want in this world without money by one of three things; beauty, mind, or force. You can be the wealthiest man in the world, that won't get you women. There are plenty of bozos with bread. There's an epidemic of them. 'Cheese' attracts 'hood rats.' Diamonds and capital attract gold diggers. Experience will teach you plenty. Body language, what's not said, what is said, what to listen to, what not to listen to. What to observe and what not to observe. When to speak and when not to. Why do you think it's extremely difficult for highly intelligent, alpha women to find mates? They either one, dumb themselves down to settle for less, or two, remain single. Looks, nor money is a factor. Don't use what you don't have! Don't be what you aren't. If you're not a genius, do not pretend to be. Remember, intelligent people can play dumb, dumb people cannot play intelligent.

You can quote Socrates all day, you still do not sound intelligent. Inconsistency and the lack of you keeping up with a persona will eventually get you exposed. If you are not a dominant, nor dominant, don't be that. If you're not a thug, do not pretend to be. If you're a comedian, stick to telling jokes, impersonating other things will not work for you. If you are not a smooth talker, don't be that. If you are a person with the gift of gab, then use that. If you don't like tattoos, don't attempt to begin to get any, some hurt and it's a commitment, patience and time to invest you know you don't have. You want muscles, don't just do it for a season. If you are shy, be shy. Use what works for you, not what works for him.

What works for the next man will never work for you. Some men have a natural comfort around the opposite sex. They get along with women, and women love them. If a woman is a basket case. If she is a handful, she will reward you for being patient with her. It places you in a category other man will never touch, knowing you can handle her at her best and worst. Knowing you can handle her like no other man can handle her, places you in the unforgettable platform. Last but not least....no woman truly loves a man she cannot learn from.

Why Dominant men are chased by women

KINGS chase royalty, loyalty, respect. Not what is between a woman's legs. Women behave like the men who they are associated with. A man's character is determined by the woman or women he chooses and is/are associated with. Ladies must be conscious of this the next time they have a desire to post half naked pictures or twerking their cheeks on social media. If you're not a stripper or a model, does it make sense to engage in such activity? We live in a visually dominated world, where individuals are visually dominated and brainwashed. Most of you do not mind paying top dollar for quality. However, you grant basic, regular, non-quality people access to you for a discount? You women realize you are not filet mignon, lobster, broccoli, or asparagus right? You women are Burger King and McDonald's. You are not 'rare,' some of you aren't even medium rare or well done. Men will view you as great to have sex with, but never to be committed to. This results in leaving you to remain single, if these are the activities you will constantly engage in. Some people are just not ready for you yet. Perhaps, they never will be! A Ferrari or Lamborghini knows its value, that's why there are no commercials for them. And it will never lower its price, because Honda is.

It doesn't matter how tough or cold a woman is, there are certain words which melt her heart. Women desire mental stimulation, no matter what type of woman she is. Anything you provide a woman, she enhances ten times greater. You give a good woman $500, she'll turn it into $5000. You give her groceries, she'll make you a meal. You give her security, protection, assurance, honesty, she'll give you loyalty. You give her great sex, she might give you her mind. You give her words, she will give you her soul. Men simply believe, the only way inside her is through her genitalia. If you can penetrate her mind, you will penetrate her body WELL. If your 'consciousness' can penetrate her body well, you can influence her cerebral. If he is not feeding your mind, how is he touching your soul?! The mind is required just as much massaging as the body. Enticing neurons, synapses. Transmitting of energy, vibrations and frequency to one another.

A massive throbbing vocabulary has a greater chance of 'filling' her cerebral. Shoving your enormous brilliance between her begging subconscious. Reaching beyond her pituitary gland, inspiring her thoughts and ideas to burst everywhere. The bigger the consciousness, the more chances you have to seduce her. Taste her thought process, unravel the intricate and hidden riddles. Read 'between' those lines. Explore through the cosmos, and against time. The deeper and deeper you go, the sweeter it becomes. That intricate intellectual intercourse. But, I'm greedy, I want to see and feel more. Your fears, your passion, ideas, insecurities. Show me everything no one else sees. The side of you no one else knows. Impress me with your honesty, courage, loyalty, art, energy, creativity, vibrations and frequency.

A woman believes power is between her legs? Ha, I'll make a liar out of her. Power is between her cerebrum. Her cerebral cortex, as you touch her neurons and synapses. When you touch them, you make her body do what you want it to do. It is now fully aware who's its king. It moves when you move, like a puppet on string. If I could summarize Dominance, I would say, it is old school relationship and values. However, what it entails transcends the parameters of what a basic, traditional man has to offer. A real Dominant man can grant him and his partner access into a psychological, emotional and physical space, others are not privileged of. Sharing secrets, fears, doubts, etcetera. A bunch of eccentric, passionate individuals whom require a connection so deep and intense. We engage in everything HARD! These true sapiosexual Dominant men, do not recognize these ones in this new generational era. They love phones calls, they adore notes, they love dates, they appreciate face to face interactions, they vibe off connection, frequency and energy. They love books, music and poetry.

How to be a Dominant man: Training yourself to win

Communication is artistic to me. Voice tonality, phone calls not just text, hugs and love not just sex. Hand written love notes, spiritual depth. Word play, very passionate. The greatest actor of all time, Denzel Washington once said, 'never confuse movement with progress, because you can run in place and not be going anywhere. When you're up, bring one up with you. Then another. Teach one. Inspire one. Don't just strive to make a living. Strive to make a difference!' Women must stop lying to men to get men to like them for who they are not. And men must stop lying to women to obtain something from them they truly do not care about or don't know how to handle. Men must stop acting like they've never had women before. Women must act as if they were raised by humans and not wolves. It's never about having power, it's about what you do with power. Control is lovely. Power is priceless. However, as priceless as power is, the irony is no one truly has it. Daddy issues, emotional trauma, utilizing platforms as a defense mechanism. Unhappy, but trying so hard to show the world you are. Low self-esteem and on a course of extreme self-destruction. Intelligence and being smart are two different things. Educated and intelligence do not correlate with one another. The amateurs always attempt to follow the alphas/the real/inspiring/influential to make themselves also look like the same. In reality, they won't be able to hold that up for too long, cause that's not who and what they truly are. It won't be something consistent. Real recognizes real. Fake recognizes real as well, however, real does not recognize fake.   A woman will post a half-naked picture and receive many comments and likes, with the misconception that those are her real fans. A woman can post a photo fully clothed, and won't receive as much. But what if it's the same woman? Those are your true fans? Do they support anything else you promote, or just show up when you display skin? I bet things would appear a lot different if women were promoting positive, inspirational and motivation quotes. Taking videos of them cooking and cleaning, or reading a book out loud. A true Dominant man will only want real substance. Not something anyone can purchase or entertain.   Some people aren't aware of the real definition of king and queen. Some women are only built for one type of man, and some men are only built for one type of woman. Some women attract men from the hood, corporate Wall Street men, dominant men, kings, etc. Some men attract hood rats, corporate women, dominant, queens, or aggressive women, etc. Then there are some whom specifically attract one type. Why? Well, their idiosyncrasies, that's why. Their appearances, that's why. Their habits, their patterns. Their behaviors. And most of you want people to not judge you based off of your social media? How you dress and how you behave? Okay, so, you should go to a job interview with shorts and a tank top and you're entitled to be mad when you don't get the job? People don't care about what's on your resume. They judge based off your vibrations, energy and frequency, not just your words. The interaction is vital! Having a good understanding of all these things, help to enable what a real dominant man stands for, and respect.

No woman will ever fall in love with a man she cannot learn from. No man fully falls for a woman that does not give her all to him. Mind, body and soul. Be conscious of who you share your sacred sexual energy with. What I do and teach, is not associated with inadequate development.

I do not help men get with women to hit and quit. I do not help women engage with men, where they are closed off, dismissive and apprehensive. I encourage connection. Love. Passion. Intimacy (and I don't mean just physical). Connect with her soul first. Taste her thought process. Witness how she blossoms with intelligence.

Let's be honest, women love Dominance. They are designed that way. Outsmart her. Intrigue her. Make her think. Challenge her. Trust me, you will be on her mind all day. Chemistry is when you can touch her mind, and by that you will set her body on fire. Your touch will heat up her flesh faster than a sun beaming on a barren land. Good sex is not enough, if you cannot have a deep and enticing conversation afterward, naked while you eat snacks. That's true intimacy. You want to attract what you desire? Be the energy that you want to attract. You are made of stars. The atoms of our bodies are traceable to stars that manufactured them in their core and explode these enriched ingredients across our galaxies, billions of years ago. This is the reason we are biologically connected to every other living thing in the world. We are chemically connected to all molecules on earth. We are automatically connected to all the atoms in the universe. Certain people and their toxic energies can block you from expanding, elevating, and vibrating higher than your own expectations. Like I said above, and I will reiterate, be conscious of who you share your sacred sexual energy with. Energy is contagious. We as humans pick up on vibrations.

Another soul can be healing or detrimental to your soul. Then you carry that energy, whether it's good or bad towards wherever or whomever you go on to. In order for you to be able to make someone else happy, you need to be happy with yourself. Your life. Your spirit. Your body. Your mind. Ninety percent of human communication is non-verbal. So, that means ten percent of people are not saying anything. Body language, eye contact, posture, the way people walk, their tone, has plenty to do with their energy and vibrations. The universe is asking, "show me a new vibration and I will show you miracles." The mind is above space and time.

Deciding not to complain, you will be compensated with intuition. In religions they refer to it as, 'spirit.' In science they refer to it as, 'energy.' Part of healing, and growth is experience. Letting go, allows you to move and receive. When was the last time someone touched you other than your body? Good sex involves the body. But, great intimacy begins in the mind. Nowadays, no one knows how to converse anymore. Social media has taken over. Everyone is busy. No one has time or care to drown in another. Put in work to know one another, and it gets harder as we get older.

A woman will always love a man more from what she has learned from him, versus the expensive things he can buy her. Sex is an exchange of energy. It is emotional. Sexual chemistry now becomes very powerful. Great relationships are built upon mutual respect, trust, selflessness. Where there is trust, there is respect, where there is respect, there is attractions. Without attractions, there is no relationship or at least not a real one. This is why there are plenty of one-night stands.

You could meet someone, and your body reacts to them. Not your mind or soul, but your body. It is magnetic. Sexual chemistry can be short term or long. It all depends what you have outside of that. By 'that', I mean an emotional connection as well. The person might just be physically compatible with you so well, that this is all you allow him or her to do. There is no talking. There is no conversing. This is short lived. Some people have a sexual preference, perhaps race, built, physique preference, an appearance where they know they are more compatible with. This is what inspires "unfaithful relationships." This is what creates them. You really can't control who you find sexy. Who you find irresistible. You perhaps have a husband or wife, and you have a great emotional connection, but weak sexual chemistry. Perhaps it's the other way around. Perhaps none at all.

Some people build this chemistry through, trial and error. Sexual chemistry. Reciprocated chemistry is the answer. This is what you feel when you are sitting beside them or even just gazing at them across the room. Sometimes the pheromones are so powerful, that it actually pulls you towards them like a magnetic force. There is a magic in the air and it is an unmistakable euphoric feeling. How often does it happen? Not as often as one would think. What are the signs? There is an overwhelming urge to be close and touch them. It is like an electric current that is pulling you into them.

It is not always at the right moment, it can be with someone who is out of bounds, but it is an undeniable feeling, and hard to ignore! Nervousness that you are not used to feeling. An arousal, an amazing urge to kiss them right there on the spot. That you are willing to be intimate with them as quickly as possible despite your strong morals. Certain people that are in relationships require distance from one another, or this occurs. Their scent is overly alluring and draws you closer. You are drawn into their eyes and have trouble focusing on what they are saying. If you are both single this is great but if not, it can be the catalyst in many relationship problems! Due to the magnitude of the electrical current, some people tend to step over their boundaries. Acting first and dealing with the repercussions later.

Does age make a difference in how a person looks at chemistry? Yes! As a person matures, so does their awareness. They may become more selective or intuitive due to some of the mistakes they have made in the past, and now when they feel it, they know it! (Some people can have a sexual relationship without the love and passion which is a "friends with benefits" rapport).

In your younger years you are sexually peaking, everything is experimental and not so much about chemistry. Everyone looks good and feels good for a while, until you start to differentiate with new emotions. In high school, most crushes for myself were experiments with an attraction. No one is thinking about a future yet. Ask your partner what the word "chemistry" means to them? Keep that alive and work with it continuously.

Many couples let it fade by allowing other daily forces to replace passion. Nurturing each other first should be a priority. Think back to when you first became a couple, everything else in your life took second place. Keeping the chemistry alive will keep your relationship alive! Many parents today think it is selfish to get a babysitter and have a date night. Many older parents fall into this trap, because they have waited so long to have a family and now make it all about the children. This is a big mistake. Is it better for the kids to come from a divorced family, because the couple who made the kids forgot how to love each other?

Physical. Mental. Emotional. Spiritual. How great it is when you have it all. If you get lucky that is. In my life, I have never witnessed a bond, a sexual chemistry, an emotional, deep connection, intimacy stronger than a passionate Man and a loving, giving woman. You are the universe. We do not always get what we pray for, what we wish for. We obtain what we justly deserve and earn. To alter the universe, alter your thoughts. Because, the only universe you will ever know, is in your mind.

Ignoring your passion is slow suicide. Never ignore what your heart pumps for. Build your career around your lifestyle, not your lifestyle around your career.

Sex, the spiritual aspect. When a man enters your womb what type of energy and subconsciousness does he have? Is he bitter, is he happy? Does he love himself, does he love you? Is he a positive or negative thinker? When a lady makes love to you, is she blessing you or cursing you? Is she bitter, is she happy? Does she love herself, or you? Sex is a ritual of exchanging energies, thoughts emotions and spirits. During sex you become a spiritual sponge for the consciousness and energy of that other person.

For example, a good orgasm is satisfying, but a great orgasm can be a revelation of your deepest being, unfolding the truth of who you are in ecstatic communication with your lover. In deep orgasm, if you are aware, you will know for the first-time what ecstasy is. Otherwise you have only heard the word. You have not known its meaning. Only in deep orgasm if you are aware, if your flame of awareness is burning bright, will you be able to know that sex is not just sex. Sex is the outermost layer. Deep inside is love, and even deeper than, is prayerfulness. And deepest is Godliness itself. Sex can become a cosmic experience, then it is tantra. Sex plus awareness, and something tremendous starts changing.

When you are evolving to your higher self, the road seems lonely. But you're simply shedding energies that no longer match the frequency of your destiny.

When you love what you do, it's never feels like Work. Some people have knowledge and keep it to themselves. That's because, they're selfish. Many people have no idea why they are on this earth. I know why I'm here. I'm a healer. I was never here to take part, I was here to take over. To teach, to guide, to open eyes and awaken souls. What's a soul? It's like electricity lights up a room and enlightens others as you come around. You are that electricity. We are receivers and transmitters of energy. We constantly send out frequency and vibrations of energy that attract or repel vibrations.

Everything you do today, is preparing you for tomorrow. A scientist will read dozens of books in his lifetime, but still believe he has a lot to learn. A religious person barely reads one book, and will think they know it all.

Some people are dead, and some are awakened. The reason many people are not on my level or the level of those that think and behave like me, is because they are dead. Their flesh may be on earth, but their minds and spirits are dead.

Only a few of us in the world, think like this. People are supposed to live extremely long. Very long. Like 3000 years old and so on. You ever read in the Bible how long these people actually lived? Yes, the Bible was written like over and over and over to suit lies and personal beliefs, however, the reason people do not live that long anymore is because of foods they put in their bodies, things they are watching that is in their minds. Programmed in their cells in their cerebral, and their pituitary gland. Why do you think people die? Cells, you have to have a certain number of cells.

Why do you think some kids are born with mental disabilities? Chromosomes. How do you know these mandatory vaccinations aren't doing more harm than good to children? If you're going to waste ten minutes, or an hour of your life on social media, make it worth it. Sustain something that is useful. You know the irony of social media? It's built for us to be social, but, has made us anti-social.

You know why a pretty woman won't give a regular man the time of day in life? Because, insecure men fill their head with nonsense. They patronize these women. Cater to them all day, suck up to them. Fill their DMs, likes, comments, etc. All that goes to these women's heads. Without social media, a lot of men and women would not have confidence, and their self-esteem would be low. Relationships would workout. Communicating efficiently would have a higher percentage.

People are brain washed, you work all week, just to wait for the weekend to go to the club? Every weekend? I have to be honest, one thing I dislike on a woman's page, is when her page is full of selfies. That's a selfish person (but, that just my opinion). There's no quotes, nothing intellectual on there. Just her looks, she appears shallow and vain. If she is half naked all the time, she's constantly seeking attention. If she's not a model or a fitness enthusiast, those pictures should be for her man.

For many it is very hard understand this, and insecure men will never be able to grasp this concept. Yes, I tend to judge people based on their posts, statuses and what they display on social media. If I was your potential boss, and you wanted to work for my company, would you hire you if you were me? A man doesn't owe you anything just because you're a female or you look good or your accomplishments. You still need to prove yourself. Show him why you're worthy, something that should be treated special.

The best thing you can do is mold your spirit. Not so much your mind. Your spirit is forever. Soul mates never break up. For example, a woman can tell me, "I'm leaving." She's never leaving me. And I don't mean it like, I'm going to physically restrain her. I know how I am, when I'm invested in someone deep, I emotionally and psychologically connect with her. She may find another partner, but it would never work out. Because, even if her flesh is there, her spirit is fighting to come find me. That's true soul touching. I don't have to tell her, "I'm the best." Her soul speaks it loud and clear.

Have you ever seen Mortal Kombat? There is a powerful evil warlock, a demonic shape shifter who absorbs the living souls of those he defeats, in order to maintain his youth and power, and is able to change his appearance. Including by morphing into other characters while retaining their abilities and moves in battle. "Your soul is mine!" he bellows, then he snatches your soul. People don't need to be saved or rescued. They need knowledge of their own power and how to access it. We all should have powers. Telekinesis. Telepathy, psychic ability. X-ray vision, etc....just like the comic books and movies we see. There are foods, and things that brain washes and programs us, that defeated that. Some people are dead, they aren't awakened. That's why, a woman will never truly love a man she cannot ever learn from. Sex is a healing and bonding experience for both parties. Let words touch her in places, hands have yet to embrace.

Seduce her mind, there's no way her body won't follow. No way she won't give you her essence. Find her soul, she's yours forever. Penetrating her pituitary gland first, rearranging her uterus second, Dominating her soul third. Loving her heart fourth.

If you ever come across a woman saying, "I don't love, I never made love (I find that to be crazy, because they are women. Whom are born to be caring, loving, nurturing naturally) or "all men _____, and _____" fill in the blanks. What she's saying is what she's attracting. That's the reality. Second, if she's never loved properly, it's because she's never learned how to love properly from a man.

A man is not going to learn how to love a woman from a man. A woman is not going to learn how to love a man properly from a woman. She's going to learn how to love a man, from a man. Love is a power. Love is healing. Do you know your sexual power? Your spiritual power? Your physical power, and your mental power?

You cannot perceive what you are not a vibrational match to. A serious woman, when she finds someone who calms her spirit, and quiets her busy thoughts, will love you so fiercely, it will defy even her own logic or reasoning. Our sexuality is not something that can be used for the enhancement of an intimate relationship, for physical pleasure, or procreation. It can also be used for personal transformation, physical and emotional healing, self-realization, and spiritual growth, and as a way to learn about all of life and death. An honest, sexually knowledgeable woman, or group of women, is a divine and extremely powerful force that not only can inspire other women, but also has the potential to contribute to the well-being of all life on earth.

Everything in life is balanced. Everything physical (matter/energy) goes back and forth in balanced circles, cycles, or the equivalent. Positive and negative forces moving in balance are the physical universe. So taking care of your energy is key. Here are some crucial things to take note of:

One in three people are overweight. One in six has learning disabilities. One in nine has asthma. One in ten has ADHD, and one in twelve has food allergies. One in twenty has seizures, one in fifty-four males has autism, and one in eighty-eight people has autism. Fifty percent of all children have chronic illness or are overweight.

This is the new normal in our country. If you are not concerned yet, then you should be.

An excellent method for cleansing your energy is shower meditation. Every time you take a shower, visualize washing away your stress and anxiety.

Concentrate on the feel of the water upon your skin. Envision the power of the water washing away your negative thoughts. Feel sadness, regret, anger and depression washing right off of you. Let it all go down the drain. You will start to feel lighter and much clearer.

Chapter 5 -Proper planning, results and great performance

Intensity, integrity and intelligence are the 3 I's and the keys to life. Be proactive no one is going to give you anything in life, work and take what you desire. When you plan you will never be left out. Never be late, never fail, and you'll always be on top of the game. You must be disciplined in your mind, body, and your emotions; you must have the strength to be able to control all 3. Discipline is the prime factor of domination, it's not 20% or 50%. Discipline is 100%. If you are disciplined in your focus, you can dominate in all that you choose to do. You cannot just switch it on and off either, make it so it's on at all times. You either have it or you don't.

You should have a "take what you want" attitude. Having a dynamic personality allows you to connect with all types of people, you don't have to worry about putting the needs of others first. This isn't a bad thing. When it comes to your aspirations, dreams, career, you should put your needs first regardless of what people think or want for you. Don't follow your dreams, live your dreams.

There is no such thing as being over educated, or overdressed. People take notice, they see the difference, they sense electricity in the air as soon as you walk into the place. Instinctively you sit up a little bit straighter, you fix your hair, you smooth down your clothes or straighten your tie, you automatically want to be better when you're in better company, and confidence is key. It's how you act, it's how you plan. Knowing you're the best, but never being overly cocky. The way you dress shows how you plan. The way you think is how you plan. The way you speak is how you plan. Your whole demeanor is how you plan, it shows how you are proud of who you are. What you look like, and the vibes you emit to those around you. No one is more conscious of your own physical appearance than you. If you don't look good, you won't feel good. If you're constantly late, you don't have a plan. If you're constantly making mistakes you don't have a plan.

We all have our strength and weaknesses, but sharpen your weakness to perfection. There is always room for improvement. But never focus too long on flaws. Acknowledge them, fix them and move on, never allow negativity to hold you back. If you start to drown in negativity you will begin to focus on the bad and not the good. This is redundant and does not help you in your growth, or the growth in those around you.

As a Leader you need to be strong and determined, you need to have the strength and confidence in yourself and for those that don't have those traits, so they can see you out and know that you will support them in abundance. For example, with me; the night before I plan. I plan my clothes by ironing them; I pick out what shoes I'm going to wear. Whether I lay it out or keep mental documentations, so now when I wake up I shower, brush my teeth and then I already know what I'm going to wear, what I'm going to make for breakfast, and therefore I am ready for the day.

Preparation is key. Only you can do you, no one else. Always strategize; always plan your attack in your daily life, it's simple. If you are prepared, then you will succeed. Be methodical and meticulous in how you approach things, with how you spend your time; don't waste it on things that will get you nowhere fast. I always make sure I am doing something to make me better every single day. The only person you have to beat is the person you were yesterday. You are your own competition. Between work, clients, and my busy daily schedule, you will always find me reading, writing or finding ways on how to improve something that I am not 100 percent happy with.

I don't waste my time, I make time. Time is money, and wasted time is wasted money. You can't get that back. Only boring people get bored. To get yourself motivated you need incentive, ask yourself what you want the most and set goals to achieve this. You need to make sure you surround yourself around the right people.

People that inspire you, that push you to achieve those goals, People tend to always surround themselves around other successful people. You must always appreciate the good people you have around you. You should always want to impact those around you. If you surround yourself with the right caliber of people, you will not want to disappoint them; it's a good form of motivation. To make sure you hold yourself accountable for all that you do. How you treat people is a huge representation of yourself. Being great is being prepared, to be great does not require total transformation in your character or drastic improvements on your physical improvements, it is just simply psychological. It's in the grasp of anyone willing to master it. All that is required of you is that you look at the world differently. Like a good general they plan and strategize. It is the effort that you put in the display of "you care" and there is no substitution for hard work. You will reap the benefits of the hard work down the line. You're not going to settle for excuses.

The only expectations from yourself will be set to high standards whether you exceed them or not. If you ever want to be good at something, you have to do it consistently, practicing what you've learned. To be taught a lesson you need to experience it. What makes my methods effective? Passion and intensity!

There are 7 advantages to proper planning

Organize your thinking. First, the planning process forces you to organize your thinking and identify all the key issues that must be dealt with if you are ultimately going to succeed.

Plan your day and actions accordingly. Set aside the time you need to properly coordinate your schedule and time. Remain focused, and do not deviate from that schedule.

Identify potential flaws in your approach. A good plan, thoroughly discussed and evaluated, enables you to identify flaws and errors that could prove fatal to your business later on. It enables you to ask, 'what if?' questions. For example, 'What are the worst possible things that could happen if you were to take a particular course of action.'

Follow up and locate weaknesses in your plan and come up with corrective actions. A great asset of proper planning is that it helps you to identify weaknesses in your plan and make provisions to compensate for those weaknesses in them. You can identify a 'fatal flaw' that would lead to the failure of an entire business. This is only possible by going through the planning process.

Identify what your strengths are, and come up with opportunities to improve success. What this does is it enables you to identify strengths and potential opportunities that you can take advantage of to increase the likelihood of success. It very likely that you won't even realize certain mistakes in things you have done previously. Properly planning your agenda will alleviate many mishaps in the future.

Make certain you are focusing your efforts on what is important. Many times we bombard ourselves with unnecessary things that are not relevant to our main agenda. Choose your strategy wisely before moving forward.

Pace yourself. This is not a race. Being accurate and precise is more important to your bottom line, then speed.

While your plans may change, hopefully it's the act of planning that provides you some stability and a firm foundation to propel your way forward.

Strategic planning for business

Within the business and corporate structure, organizations have an entirely different set of rules they adhere to and follow. The objective of the business owners is to operate a smooth and carefully run business that they can return a good profit from.

A successfully run organization does not happen by chance, but is rather a result of careful planning where objectives are clearly set. The aim of every firm is to achieve certain goals, and these have to be identified. After identifying the goals for the organization, a course of action has to be drawn. This is a process which requires the involvement of strategists within that particular company. Creating a well thought out plan is paramount to having an efficiently run business. Strategize your profit margins, your five-year plan, and even an exit strategy for loss of profits. Carefully projecting your numbers can produce great results.

Another way to take advantage of proper business planning is that the resources are allocated according to the available budget. Given such a situation, there will be little chance of wasting resources through embarking on unplanned activities. Always focus on the set goals you have in place, and utilize your energies into those projections. Your profits will be more likely to bring in a return, when used wisely.

Strategic planning also helps to eliminate duplication of duties within the company. Through scheduling, the tasks are allocated in a manner that allows all members of an organization to know their roles. Delegation is important here, as people need to understand their position, and what they bring to the company. Planning things out deliberately helps to create a smooth working environment for your people.

The success of business can only depend on how well and organized the leaders are, that are in the head position of operations. If the leaders of the organization are able to motivate their subordinates, employees will also put optimum effort into their actions which can promote business success. Employees need to be treated as valuable assets to the organization. All the work in an organization is done by the employees; hence they deserve recognition for their efforts.

There are many important elements of running a company successfully, and one very key principle, is the involvement of the employees in the decision-making process. If the members are given the encouragement to contribute towards the decision-making process, they will become part of the organization and they can proudly identify with it. Employees that are acknowledged often are motivated in making the company a more successful place to work in. Making them feel appreciated can directly impact your business.

In this day and age, businesses are very competitive, and thrive on building a culture that people want to be a part of. Measures ought to be in place for them to be viable in the operations. Failure to do so can negatively impact the viability of the organization. Basically, business success is not an overnight event, but a process which requires proper planning.

What is the definition of the 6-P rule?

Properly preparing your agenda, helps to prevent poor performance. It alleviates disorder and the possibility of disorganization.

What does that 6-P rule mean? "Prior Proper Planning Prevents Poor Performance", what does that mean? It is the definition of being prepared. Creating a pathway for yourself that negates any room for lack of production.

It begins with you. How you start your day will determine how your energy and production is used. Having an organized and well though out plan of action, can boost your motivation and ingenuity.

So, what does it mean to properly plan a day prior to beginning it?

Many individuals think that waking up and forming your agenda is the best way to move forward. However, this is the least effective mode of action that is successful. You need to plan your agenda the day before, in order to properly execute it the right way. Formulate how your day will go, from the morning to the evening. Prepare room for the unseen, (things out of your control) and map out a strategy to handle it. If you do this often enough, your plan may not be perfect, however it will be well conducted.

Advantages of following an agenda

Research suggests that 90% of your time can be saved every day, if you spent 10% of your time planning your day prior to getting started with the day's work. This can be done, only with a well thought out agenda from the day before.

Execute the plan

Delivering a well thought out and successful agenda, can be challenging for most people. Most people are never clear about what they want and that is why it takes a long time for them to do anything. Thinking and strategy takes persistence, and patience. Something we discussed previously. And distractions must be eliminated in order to see this through. When you plan every single day before hand, you actually are giving your mind a clear vision, an idea of what you want to do and accomplish for the rest of the day and this makes it easier for your mind to cooperate with you and help you accomplish it all.

Remaining focused and logical

Starting your day with an agenda you already prepared, gives you a sense of purpose. Being able to move and operate with strategy and focus, creates a feeling of success when you are able to complete each task on your list.

Hierarchical planning

With this type of strategic planning, you are dealing with different time expectations, and outcomes. It is very important to plan your goals for the long term. Always set expectations for five-year and ten-year plans, when pertaining to profit margins and returns. However, when you are setting agendas and guidelines for the immediate future, you need a weekly plan. Organizations generally have a weekly goal of objectives and numbers they expect their people to meet, in order to accomplish the yearly and long-term agendas. This works out more smoothly, and allows leaders to properly train and see various areas needed for improvement.

This can be completed by creating a weekly plan for the next week, at the end of each current week. This very much like preparing your daily agenda for yourself the day before. Only now, you are considering the goals and objectives of other individuals as well. Weekly plans are best designed by working with your head managers. Having a weekly meeting of where everyone is currently at as far as numbers, or profits. Creating the weekly agenda should be comprised where all leaders within the head departments running your organization are all on the same page, as far as expectations. Starting small (weekly) will allow you to accomplish the bigger (yearly) long term goals.

What this does is that, it gives you a clear sense of purpose and an idea of what you have to do. When you hold yourself accountable to this plan and these goals that you have written down, and when you are driven from the inside to really do these things to accomplish what you want, that's when the success starts happening.

The success of utilizing the 6-P rule

Proper planning is not difficult to do, as long as you understand how to make it work for you. For example, if you are accustomed to doing something every single day for the past ten years, it would be very challenging to break the monotony of that cycle of routine. However, incorporating the use of the 6-P rule will help to bring order and structure into your life.

You can begin in small steps. Write one thing you want to get done the next day. Write it down on a piece of paper. Then the next day, make an effort to get that one item off of that list. Crossing it off the list will give you a sense of great satisfaction. A feeling of accomplishment. If you are not used to doing this, then your mind will be greatly impacted by the rushing desire to accomplish more. You will then see yourself creating more little items, and getting things done, in a timelier fashion.

The Importance of Discipline

Having the desire for change is never enough. You have to want to make it happen for yourself. And understand that it may not miraculously begin overnight.

Keep in mind that this is simply a guideline. If you make the effort to actively begin changing your routine, and planning a successful strategy for yourself, you will begin to see amazing results over time.

Always remember the 6-P rule. And use it to your advantage. Prior Proper Planning Prevents Poor Performance.

Chapter 6 – Passion Changes Everything

When you find your passion, it changes everything. If you're a passionate individual everything for you is different. When you find your niche, you become a master at your craft. You are great at whatever you enjoy. When you love something all you care about is that. You are dedicated to it. Committed. You apply your mind body and soul into it. You can't go a day without thinking of it or engaging in it. Passion is ambition. It is drive, it is heart, it is excitement, it is love, it is emotions, it is art, it is strength, and it is not a hobby. Regular people will call it obsessed, we call it passion.

Being passionate is being invested. Time, effort, cost, passion, is a combination of love and hatred. Because along with the obsession comes a need for perfection. Passion is not something you can go and switch on and off or even tone it down. Passion is associated with energy, drive, enthusiasm, limitless motivation and push. Find your passion and embrace it, master it, perfect it, love it, eat sleep breathe it, passion allows us to overcome obstacles, whether those obstacles are actual or imaginary, passion allows you to overcome them. I see the world as a place of infinite potential.

The power of passion also enables us to have self-confidence, trust ourselves and to take the risks required to live every day to its fullest. Living with passion is about having the courage to express your thoughts, opinions, convictions and your love for life. That love for life comes because you live a life by design, not by default. Following your passion enables you to do so. That is the power of passion! Dare to imagine what living a life filled with passion is like, dare to imagine the possibilities, dare to live your dream, and dare to actually search for what you love. Know that it is not only a possibility, but also a probability to live with passion...if you have the confidence! With confidence and passion, anything is possible. I hope you'll challenge yourself to live with passion and take risks and take action. So that you too can LIVE LIFE FULLY! Here are a few tips for you to help discover what you are passionate about:

1 – Determine what you are good at

What are your skills, talents and gifts? There are things that you are naturally good at and enjoy doing. Often people forget about things they excel at because they come so naturally. Think back to when you were younger, as far as you can, to jobs, projects, and hobbies. Maybe you've always been a good writer, drawer, organizer, creator, builder, teacher, and friend? Spend an hour thinking about this and make a list of all your answers.

2 – Determine what excites you

Is it a part of your job that excites you? Is it a hobby, a side job, something you volunteer your time doing? Maybe it's something that you do as a spouse, a parent or a friend. Maybe it's something you haven't done in a while. Spend an hour thinking about this and make a list of all your answers.

3 – What do you spend hours reading about?

When I get passionate about something, I'll read about it and research it for countless hours. That's a very good indication of something you could be passionate about. Oprah once said:

"If you don't know what your passion is, realize that one reason for your existence on earth is to find it."

Why it matters

Passion matters because it correlates with the desire and capacity to go above and beyond the call to achieve superlative goals and outcomes. It's often what separates average performers from extraordinary performers. It's not entirely different from motivation, in that it is one of the key aspects of grit.

As shown within Indeed's 2015 Talent Attraction Study, the number one concern among recruiters hiring passive candidates was lack of passion and commitment. You can have people who check all the boxes — they went to the right college, have relevant experience, and seem to have a personality that could mesh well with your team — but if they are missing genuine passion, they could easily wind up an as average or, worse, a below average hire.

The difference in ROI between average and great hires is huge, by some estimates more than a million dollars in revenue per hire over the course of an employee's stint at a company. Those are, by any measure, massive stakes.

Knowing your passion

Understanding what drives you can be the difference with what will define you. There are many instances where you will find yourself taken in by the beauty or desire for something wonderful. But does this wonderful thing make you want to get up in the morning?

Identifying passion is a bit like identifying motivation. It's about *why* not *what*. The key is to understand why someone accomplished what they did, and less about what they accomplished. Are they motivated by money, recognition, or something else entirely? Do they thrive on solving complex problems or being part of a team and helping others out? These questions are about how a recruiter can figure out how well a candidate aligns with an organization.

A recruiter could correctly identify 90% of the key skills a candidate needs to thrive in a role, but if they fail to identify a candidate's passion or lack thereof, it could still wind up a bad hire. So, it behoves recruiters to learn what kind of passions are most predictive of success in various roles on various teams.

This can be accomplished by carefully asking the right questions. Knowing what and how a person is motivated by, will aide in the selection process, and give you a better idea of the type of person you are dealing with.

These are key elements in discovering the passion behind the purpose. Questions, observation, listening and understanding. If you garner the skill in using these factors together, they will assist you in finding what drives an individual, and their true motivation.

Failure can be the turning point of success

The origin of the word passion is the latin word *pati*, which means suffering or enduring. Passion can mean many things. It brings to mind the feeling of beauty and powerful emotions derived from lust. It also holds the key to what moves the human nature and keeps us alive. But it can also mean long suffering, and the ability to bear great lengths of pain.

Human emotions are the most interchanging of any species created. We are designed to not only adapt to our environment, but we have within us the ability to change our surroundings and make it into something we can use and achieve in.

When we as individuals fail at a task or purpose, we set out to accomplish, our emotions are often entangled with doubt and disappointment. This can affect our desire to move forward. And your passion becomes your nightmare. Your dreams and aspirations seem out of reach because of setbacks that you may not have properly prepared for.

Identifying how candidates respond to failure is essential to identifying their resilience and capacity for innovation. Moreover, candidates who respond to failure by assessing and adapting are apt to see failure as an opportunity to learn and improve.

Failure can be the turning point of success, or it can become the bridge that takes you over into your next level. You must decide as an individual which statistic you will be. You can choose to allow failure to destroy your passion for life. Or, you can use it to catapult your career beyond your expectations.

Taking away the need for more

Success can be a very addictive aphrodisiac. It can become the reason you live and breathe. If success alone is your passion, then you have a serious problem. Because what will happen to your desire for life, if your success is no longer present? People that base all of their hopes and dreams on the sole basis of success, are not living their passion. They are consumed with living for the thrill of money and power. Having these things are great. And can make one feel as if they have achieved all they desire. But the problem with this, is when you take away the desire to have more.

For example, if you have accomplished all your financial goals, and have obtained more than the successful dream you have set for yourself, do you often wonder why many individuals then feel as if it is not enough? Why some people who appear to have it all, never seem quite happy or even content with their achievements?

The reason for this is the constant need for more. That is their driving passion. The inward feeling of incompletion. People who are driven by the need for more, are never satisfied with what they have. It will never matter how much success they gain, or the goals they manage to meet. They will always be left with a hunger for something they currently do not have. And this is something that will always block your true purpose in life.

Passion is not often understood, and therefore it is misconstrued as something you feel only when involved in intimacy.

Passion includes sexual desire, but it's more than that. According to Sternberg (1986), passion involves a longing for someone, which can be inclusive of sexual desire, but can also describe the emotions involved in the powerful connection between a parent and a child.

Do you need passion for long-term relationship happiness? Here's what the scientific research has to say on the question:

Is it really love or just friendship? Sternberg (1986) suggests that relationships can be mapped onto a triangle with its points defined as intimacy, commitment, and passion. Without passion, you might have a relationship high in intimacy and commitment—typically, what characterizes friendships rather than romantic couples. The ideal? A relationship characterized by the center of the triangle—consummate love—which includes intimacy, commitment, and passion.

However, passion can also be identified as believing or strongly being motivated and convicted to pursue something. It can be what drives your desires for success.

But passion also matters in sexual satisfaction. The kind of passion between two people that leads to sexual satisfaction is highly rewarding in romantic relationships, and sexual satisfaction is a strong predictor of overall relationship satisfaction, commitment, and love (Sprecher, 2002).

Passion in a relationship is important on many levels. If this very key element is missing, then the relationship will be devoid of any real intimacy or depth. There are many people that have relationships where no passion exists at all. In this instance, it is very likely the couple has a mutual agreement, when there are other factors governing the relationship. Such as business. Some people are together for simply business reasons. Or perhaps it is a relationship built on friendship alone. Either way, there are various reasons people do not have passion in the partnerships. However, if love is involved on either side, passion is needed in order to have a truly healthy and thriving one.

Whether you choose to have passion as part of your relationship or not, it is very important to understand that without it, you will have nothing more than a friendship, or co-worker. Knowing the difference when using passion in a relationship, will be the defining point of your bond together.

Intense passion during courtship may not lead to marriage. Dating couples who have discussed making their relationships permanent (e.g., marriage) tend to report more "love" than "passion"—and passion tends to be higher in those who have not discussed marriage compared to those who have (Gonzaga et al., 2006). It seems that lots of love and a dose of passion, rather than the reverse, are central features in relationships that transition to long-term partnerships.

Passion is needed. In everything. It changes the way you view things, and even directly impacts how you feel. Without passion, you will find yourself drifting through life, or relationships, with a very one-sided point of view. Leaving you unfulfilled and empty.

The passion experienced in any one relationship differs from that experienced by other couples, and even within a couple, passion tends to ebb and flow over the course the relationship. The above evidence suggests that passion is important in predicting relationship success, but that it's not the only predictor. Love, intimacy, and commitment are just as, if not more, important to relationship well-being.

Why passion matters

In life we go through a series of tests that changes our outlook on things. It shapes us into the people we are today. And builds our esteem so that we have the ability to adjust in any environment we find ourselves in. Passion is the tool we use to keep us going. The human species are driven by their desires. It determines how we dress, what we do for a living, who we date, where we live, how we eat. Everything.

Our decisions in life are directly tied into what drives us. What our passion in life is. The reason we believe we are here.

You will notice that everything you do, if it surrounds your passion, there will be lots of emotion and desire that comes along with it. Versus something that does not fuel your passion, you will have a completely different feeling and view towards it.

However, emotions can also be distracting. It's easy to personalize larger issues, and distract yourself from being effective. Having an emotional response to such a deeply emotional issue is important, but only if those emotions— anger and sadness, for example, —are being used to motivate and inspire.

Whatever inspires and motivates you, is probably in correlation with your passion. The two doesn't necessarily have to be the same. But your passion will always be the driving factor of all that motivates you.

Inspiration helps to bring your passion to life. In most cases, as children, we find ourselves inspired by an adult or event that later leads us to live a life of passion, driven to achieve the results that inspired us to move forward. Passion will always matter. It helps defines you and those moments of indecision, where you discover the difference between dreams and desires.

Follow your passion, not the fame

What drives you, and what you will work for, are two completely different things. Understand the reason behind what it is you do.

If you have a career, how did you pursue it? Was it obtained through hard work and education? Did you get up each morning driven to accomplish your goals? Or did you obtain it because your uncle owns the company? And if so, do you even really care to be there, or even like what you do?

Many people who choose careers that don't make them happy will tell you that they would all do it differently if they had the chance. You only have one life, so don't waste it working somewhere you hate just because of the money and position.

Become more passionate about the work you are doing

Living your dreams is the ideal situation for anyone. However, many people don't get to choose that option. But regardless of your circumstances, you should always do something that is as closely related to your passion as possible. In everything you do, do it with life and passion.

You can relate more to the work and come up with better ideas

Being in an atmosphere where you are working towards something you love and enjoy doing, can go a long way to making your life a happier one. You can do a better job, and even give a more pleasant experience when you are passionate about what you do. Others will also be able to tell the difference when they see someone that is happy where they work.

Work should never feel like it's forced upon you

When you value money over your overall health and your passion, you will find yourself in an endless cycle of misery. Work no longer becomes a career or a journey, but more of a taxing nuisance on your mind and body that has to get done.

Every day that you go to work with this mindset you begin to hate your job more and more. While many people feel that they must work hard to retire and have money to enjoy themselves, what's the point of enjoying yourself in your later years when you spent your life being miserable?

No matter how much money you make, nothing will help you overcome the feeling of doing something you hate

There is nothing worse than doing, or living for a purpose you don't even believe in. Your attitude will begin to reflect your inward emotions, and the turmoil you struggle with inside. Especially if you are forced to be somewhere you really don't want to be. Your actions will always display your displeasure.

Having passion makes you more inclined to work later hours

This is an evident fact that is widely known for workers in the corporate world. If you love what you do, you will spend more time developing your skills at it. This is why it is important to have passion in your career.

Every industry has a busy season and without a doubt there will come a time when you will need to put in the extra hours. Do you believe it will be easier for you to work longer on something you can relate to, or something you can't stand doing?

You are willing to go above and beyond the call of duty

You will feel more than happy to oblige in fulfilling your duties above and beyond your regular work load. It will feel like a welcome addition, when you are happy to do it.

No obstacle will stop you from achieving success

When you really enjoy what you do, nothing will stop you from getting your work done. Because you are passionate about what you do, you feel unstoppable and nothing can obstruct you from achieving greatness. Your passion ignites your work, and like a rocket, it accelerates you past road blocks that may come about. Any obstacle that comes your way is accepted and fought off with a creative solution.

When your working career consumes your life

Having a career will always take up a majority of your life, and so it will be up to you to determine how it will define your environment. And your passion.

There is no way around this, so we might as well accept the cards we are dealt. Many people go about this the wrong way because they feel like work is something they have to do rather then something they can enjoy. Once you realize that your career should be something you enjoy, then you will lead a happier and fulfilling life.

You will get more fulfillment when you achieve your goals

There is nothing compared to the thrill of achieving success. Especially when you put in the time and effort, and gave your passion into living your dream. You will feel not only fulfilled, but there will be a great deal of satisfaction in knowing you not only went after your passion, you chose to make it happen.

Living your passion never means that you have to compromise in what you believe in, to do this. You can have your passion and your dream. Always strive for both.

Chapter 7 - Confidence

Most of us live this regular life that society offers, but behind closed doors, we're all different. I do not condone of the mild pleasures that society offers, I do not offer mild pleasures that society condones. Confidence exudes strength, wisdom, pride, resiliency, courage, honor, power, all without having to say one word. You witness confidence in a person's eyes, their actions, their energy, their passion, their hard work, and their love. Confidence is contagious. Someone that knows they're great at whatever they do, are 99.9 % great at whatever they do. It's that positive thinking that oozes out and makes others start to believe it also.

There is calmness to confidence, there is a control to confidence. It can be turned up at ease at any time; it has the spirit that innately commands yours. Self-confidence is the difference between feeling unstoppable and feeling scared out of your wits. It's all day every day as soon as you wake up to the time you fall back to sleep.

Your perception of yourself has an enormous impact on how others perceive you, as well as the energy you give off, and every cell in your body people pick up on. You know you're the best and others will know it as well. Perception becomes reality. What you think, you become.

The more self-confident you are, the more likelihood you will succeed in all that you do. Mind over matter, confidence is many things. Several things it is: it's asserting yourself, it's being positive, certainty. When you display plenty of confidence the universe serves you, the way you choose to think is what will occur.

Example – when you go on an interview, the interviewer will ask why you are best qualified for this job? Do not appear unsure, do not use words like "I think" words like that sink you down the river, be confident and back it up, if you're confident and back it up, people will always believe in your confidence and you. Use words "I am" "best" "I know" in your sentences, and the universe will start to work in your favor, your mouth is the tool to conquer your mind, it is also the tool to conquer other individual's minds. when you place I AM and BEST in your mind, in your words, you start to become that. Confidence displays strength and people gravitate towards strength.

Confident Alpha males tend to think very highly of themselves. They aren't always right or perfect, but they always believe in their own ability and themselves no matter what. Not embarrassed easily. Alpha males don't worry too much about other people's opinions. Masculine. Alpha males are men. They come in all shapes and sizes but have common traits: leaders, Dominant personalities, comfortable around the opposite sex, etc. Take What He

Wants Attitude. Alpha males are not jerks or rude, but they believe they are entitled, this allows them to do things and request things an ordinary person would not.

Direct and honest.

Alpha males are not afraid to speak their mind. If they need something they will tell you. They don't hide behind a lot of fluff when they are talking to you. They tell you things you might not want to hear. Social. Alpha males have a dynamic personality that allows them to connect with all types of people. Take Chances. Alpha males are risk takers (big or small). They aren't afraid to fail because they know that success comes from taking chances.

Beta Males are Nice guys.

Beta males are some of the nicest people you will ever meet. They help you when you need help; they are courteous and pleasant to be around. May Question Their Ability. Beta males lack the confidence alpha males have. There are times that beta males will second guess themselves or make excuses to not do something even though they are fully capable. They just don't always realize their potential. Worry About What Others Think. Beta males are usually restricted in life because they care too much about what other people think. This includes family, friends and strangers.

These external factors limit what a beta male does and the choices he makes in life.

Puts the Needs of Others First.

This isn't a bad thing, but beta males put the needs of others ahead of their own. They are very giving people and unselfish. Secretive. Beta males don't always make their desires known to others.

Beta males have secrets they keep to themselves including their career aspirations, dreams, and sexual desires. This is usually due to not wanting to be judged by others and may be due to lack of self-confidence. When it comes to Dominant men, or Dominants, they are Alpha. Alpha males have always captured the admiration, even jealousy, of men and the love and lust of women. Men want to be them; women want to be with them. These are the guys who act as if the world is theirs. They are always in leadership positions, in both their personal and professional lives.

They often have swollen bank accounts. They always seem to be surrounded by vast amounts of beautiful women. Confidence. In the song, "One More Chance", Biggy Smalls said: "black and ugly as ever, however, I stay coogi down to the socks, rings chain and watch". He was saying, you don't have to look cute or handsome to get a woman. If you have confidence. Smell nice, dress well, have money, you can get women. Guys use to come up to me all the time, and say, "I have to get a lot of tattoos like you. Have to get a six pack like you. Have muscles and workout like you and I'll have all the ladies." Wrong!! Beauty is of no relevance when it comes to confidence. You can have money and be desired. Some women gravitate to the ball players, the rappers, singers, men who are in control of Fortune 500 companies. These men perhaps are assertive in life, but not in the bedroom. Then again you have different type of women.

You have some women who are sapiosexuals, where they find intelligence sexy. They require a connection so deep, that it exceeds the limits of what a basic traditional relationship has to offer. Intellectual conversations will have them begging at your mercy to taunt them. These alpha males, they refuse to conform. They're the type women tell their friends about, then their friends tell their friends about him. They are unconventional. They are Dominant. They are unstoppable. They are everything that a man could wish to be. The root of the alpha male is his mindset, his unshakable confidence, mental strength, and masculinity. Or, in slang terms, he has balls. All of this having balls, and living life like an unstoppable force, comes from within. It's a mindset.

Being an alpha male is an attitude. It is from this mindset this inner alpha attitude that everything else flows. The exciting lifestyle. The money. The women. The world. Even if he doesn't have the money, he is Dominant or in charge of every aspect, everything or person around him. All men envy and desire to become alpha males.

Alpha males have balls. In the movie, "Scarface." Al Pacino playing Tony Montana said, "the only thing in this world that gives orders is balls." Alpha males exude power and authority, both in the boardroom and the bedroom. Their very presence commands respect and leaves others in awe. I have witnessed a dramatic decline in masculinity. Whether it's on social media or life. Men are becoming increasingly emasculated and less assertive, less Dominant, and much less manly.

Men are beginning to behave more like girls than they do men. At the same time, men are becoming more and more emasculated and womanly. Men are finding themselves increasingly hopeless around beautiful women, working jobs they hate, being walked all over by others, and becoming increasingly depressed. This is why, when women today stumble upon an (increasingly rare) alpha male, they are left in awe. So let's dive right in and learn to adopt that awe-inspiring alpha attitude.

I've always remembered that every time I have been at the club, a party, or social gathering, I noticed how when I walked into the room, every woman automatically turned to check me out. It didn't matter if she was married, had a boyfriend, was engaged, or in a "kind of, sort of" - relationship, they all stared. What is it about men such as us that arouse the curiosity of the opposite sex? I'll tell you. Two words: Body language. It's not just women. Often, you'll find that men turn their heads to snatch a glance also.

Some men are able to hold themselves in such a way that they bring with them an incredibly powerful presence. They are alpha to the core. Everybody turns and looks. Every time I walk into a room, people will stop what they are doing and look up and seek eye contact with me. They can feel my energy, my Scorpio aura, and the royalty in me. They can sense the wild animal in me that is caged within my body just waiting in patience to come out. They sense the electricity in the air because they know a King has walked in. Instinctively, you sit up a little bit straighter, you fix your hair up, you smooth down your clothes or straighten up your tie. You automatically want to be better when you're in better company.

My confidence is key. Confidence is how you act; it's knowing you're the best but never being overly cocky. The way I wear my clothes is a sign of my confidence. It shows I am proud of who I am and what I look like and of the vibes I know I emit to those around me. No one is more conscious of your own physical appearance than YOU are. If you don't look good, you will not feel good, and those vibes will also ooze out of you. It's simple, dress how you wish to be addressed. Life as a Dominant is all about finding out your strengths and weaknesses and sharpening them to perfection.

There is always room for improvement, but never focus too long on flaws. Acknowledge them and fix them and move forward. Don't let negativity hold you back. If you start to drown in negativity, you'll start to focus on the bad and not the good. This is redundant and does not help in your growth or the growth in those around you. As a leader, you need to be strong, and determined. You need to have the strength and confidence in yourself and for those who don't have those traits, so they can seek you out and know that you can support them in abundance.

Fitness is a huge part of my life, and it's also a huge part of self-confidence. You work out, you feel great, you act great and you are great. Working out makes you feel powerful, untouchable, magnificent. No matter how tired you are, you have to be stronger than your mind, and you need to be Disciplined. Keep focused; working out is an integral part of everyday living, especially for your health and for your mental wellbeing.

It all comes down to how mentally strong you are, and how much you want something. If you want something bad enough, nothing and no one will ever stop you. I don't accept excuses I accept results. Keep working on you. Only you can do you, no one else. Preparation is key. Always strategize. Always plan your attack in your daily life. If you are prepared, then you will succeed. Be methodical and meticulous in how you approach things, with how you spend your time. Don't waste it on stuff that will get you nowhere fast. I always make sure that I am doing something to make me better every single day. The only person you have to beat, is the person that you were yesterday. You are your own competition. Between work and clients, and my busy daily schedule, you will always find me reading, or writing or finding ways on how to improve something that I am not 100% happy with.

I don't waste my time. I make time. Time is money and wasted time is wasted money. You can't get that back. Only boring people get bored. To keep someone motivated, and I mean yourself included, you need incentive. Ask yourself, what you want the most, and set goals to achieve this. You need to make sure the right people surround you. People that inspire you, that push you to achieve those goals. Hence, why is it that those wanting to better themselves, always congregate around a Dominant/ alpha male? You must always appreciate the good people you have around you, and you should always want to impact those around you. If you surround yourself with the right caliber of people, you will not want to disappoint them. It's a good form of motivation to make sure you hold yourself accountable for all that you do. How you treat people, is a huge representation on yourself. If someone has done something good, show your appreciation, compliment him or her, and make him or her feel worthy.

A true King knows how to make those around him feel like royalty. The life of being confident is one full of success and growth of power and control. It is not for the weak. The weak never survive. But the King of the jungle will always be King, and you want to know why? Because he knows he's the best.

Building Self-Confidence

From the quietly confident doctor whose advice we rely on, to the charismatic confidence of an inspiring speaker, self-confident people have qualities that everyone admires.

Self-confidence is extremely important in almost every aspect of our lives, yet so many people struggle to find it. Sadly, this can be a vicious circle: people who lack self-confidence can find it difficult to become successful.

After all, most people are reluctant to back a project that's being pitched by someone who was nervous, fumbling, and overly apologetic.

On the other hand, you might be persuaded by someone who speaks clearly, who holds his or her head high, who answers questions assuredly, and who readily admits when he or she does not know something.

Confident people inspire confidence in others: their audience, their peers, their bosses, their customers, and their friends. And gaining the confidence of others is one of the key ways in which a self-confident person finds success.

The good news is that self-confidence really can be learned and built on. And, whether you're working on your own confidence or building the confidence of people around you, it's well-worth the effort!

How Confident Do You Seem to Others?

Your level of self-confidence can show in many ways: your behavior, your body language, how you speak, what you say, and so on. Look at the following comparisons of common confident behavior with behavior associated with low self-confidence. Which thoughts or actions do you recognize in yourself and people around you?

Confident Behavior is often Associated With Low Self-Confidence

Doing what you believe to be right, even if others mock or criticize you for it. Governing your behavior based on what other people think.

Being willing to take risks and go the extra mile to achieve better things. Staying in your comfort zone, fearing failure, and so avoid taking risks.

Admitting your mistakes, and learning from them. Working hard to cover up mistakes and hoping that you can fix the problem before anyone notices. Waiting for others to congratulate you on your accomplishments. Extolling your own virtues as often as possible to as many people as possible.

Many people are not able to admit when they are wrong. And that's the problem. It feels more powerful to always be right, but you are in fact making yourself look pathetic. Taking the higher road, and admitting when you are wrong, exudes a stronger confidence.

What Is Self-Confidence?

Too main things contribute to self-confidence: self-efficacy and self-esteem:

We gain a sense of self-efficacy when we see ourselves (and others similar to ourselves) mastering skills and achieving goals that matter in those skill areas. This is the confidence that, if we learn and work hard in a particular area, we'll succeed; and it's this type of confidence that leads people to accept difficult challenges, and persist in the face of setbacks.

This overlaps with the idea of self-esteem, which is a more general sense that we can cope with what's going on in our lives, and that we have a right to be happy. Partly, this comes from a feeling that the people around us approve of us, which we may or may not be able to control. However, it also comes from the sense that we are behaving virtuously, that we're competent at what we do, and that we can compete successfully when we put our minds to it.

Some people believe that self-confidence can be built with affirmations and positive thinking. It is believed that there's some truth in this, but that it's just as important to build self-confidence by setting and achieving goals – thereby building competence. Without this underlying competence, you don't have self-confidence: you have shallow over-confidence, with all of the issues, upset and failure that this brings.

Building Self-Confidence

I will tell you how to build this sense of balanced self-confidence, founded on a firm appreciation of reality. The bad news is that there's no quick fix, or five-minute solution.

The good news is that becoming more confident is readily achievable, just as long as you have the focus and determination to carry things through. And what's even better is that the things you'll do to build your self-confidence will also build success – after all, your confidence will come from real, solid achievement. No-one can take this away from you! To begin with, there are three steps you can use to help you in the process to building your self-confidence.

Step 1: Preparing for Your Journey

The first thing you must remember, is to always prepare for the journey you are about to embark on. Nothing worth having ever comes easy. So be prepared and set your expectations at levels you can reach.

In preparing for your journey, do these five things:

Look at What You've Already Achieved

Take the time to assess what you have already accomplished.

Put these into a smartly formatted document, which you can look at often. And then spend a few minutes each week enjoying the success you've already had.

Think About Your Strengths

Your strengths are very important. Utilizing every area can help you achieve great results, and even possibly excel in all that you do.

Think About What's Important to You, and Where You Want to Go

Next, think about the things that are really important to you, and what you want to achieve with your life.

Setting and achieving goals is a key part of this, and real confidence comes from this. Goal setting is the process you use to set yourself targets, and measure your successful hitting of those targets.

Set goals that exploit your strengths, minimize your weaknesses, realize your opportunities, and control the threats you face.

And having set the major goals in your life, identify the first step in each. Make sure it's a very small step, perhaps taking no more than an hour to complete.

Start Managing Your Mind

At this stage, you need to start managing your mind. Learn to pick up and defeat the negative self-talk which can destroy your confidence.

Commit Yourself to Success

The final part of preparing for the journey is to make a clear and unequivocal promise to yourself that you are absolutely committed to your journey, and that you will do all in your power to achieve it.

If as you're doing it, you find doubts starting to surface, write them down and challenge them calmly and rationally. If they dissolve under scrutiny, that's great. However, if they are based on genuine risks, make sure you set additional goals to manage these appropriately. Either way, make that promise.

Self-confidence is about balance. At one extreme, you have people with low self-confidence. At the other end, you have people who may be over-confident. If you are under-confident, you'll avoid taking risks and stretching yourself; and you might not try at all. And if you're over-confident, you may take on too much risk, stretch yourself beyond your capabilities, and crash badly. You may also find that you're so optimistic that you don't try hard enough to truly succeed. Getting this right is a matter of having the right amount of confidence, founded in reality and on your true ability. With the right amount of self-confidence, you will take informed risks, stretch yourself (but not beyond your abilities) and try hard.

Step 2: Setting Out the objective

Each step here is crucial. Once you take steps to execute your goals, you have to meticulously make certain you are set up to do it the right way.

Build the Knowledge You Need to Succeed

Looking at your goals, identify the skills you'll need to achieve them. And then look at how you can acquire these skills confidently and well. Don't just accept a sketchy, just-good-enough solution – look for a solution, a program or a course that fully equips you to achieve what you want to achieve and, ideally, gives you a certificate or qualification you can be proud of.

Focus on the Basic methods of success

Starting out will always seem daunting. However, you need to remain focused on the method of success. Follow the guidelines that will take you to the next level.

Start with Small Goals, then Achieve Them

Beginning with very small goals you identified in step 1, get in the habit of setting them, achieving them, and celebrating that achievement. Don't make goals particularly challenging at this stage, just get into the habit of achieving them and celebrating them.

Begin Managing Your Mind

Stay on top of that positive thinking, keep celebrating and enjoying success, and keep those mental images strong. You can also use a technique like Treasure Mapping to make your visualizations even stronger.

And on the other side, learn to handle failure. Accept that mistakes happen when you're trying something new. In fact, if you get into the habit of treating mistakes as learning experiences, you can begin to start seeing them in a positive light. After all, there's a lot to be said for the saying "if it doesn't kill you, it makes you stronger!"

Step 3: The process of Accelerating Towards Success

At this point, you can feel the difference. Within your mind and body. You can begin to feel a change within your life that will reflect the decisions you've made.

This is the time to start stretching yourself. Make the goals a bit bigger, and the challenges a bit tougher. Increase the size of your commitment. And extend the skills you've proven into new, but closely related arenas.

Keep yourself grounded – this is where people tend to get over-confident and over-stretch themselves. And make sure you don't start enjoying cleverness for its own sake.

Remember to remain humble. Over confidence can get you off track. Stay focused on what got you to this point, and never lose sight of that.

Key Points to remember

Self-confidence is needed in almost every aspect of our lives, and people who lack it can find it difficult to become successful.

These facts are the main things that contribute to self-confidence: self-efficacy and self-esteem. You can develop it with these three steps:

Prepare for your journey.

Setting out the objective.

Accelerating towards success.

Being on top of your goals, and planning your journey of confidence, can be the most rewarding experience you will encounter.

Chapter 8 - Love conquers

Everyone has their own definition of what love is, no matter what their definition is, love is still a verb. You show love and you display love. The old saying is true love conquers all, it is unconditional, and it can be rough, kind or gentle. If we would start to believe in each other, I think this world would be a better place, only way to eradicate hatred is to induce love. Love is a force of nature, however, as much as we may desire we cannot command, demand, or take away love, any more than we can command the moon and stars to come and go accordingly at our whim.

We may have the ability to change the weather, but we do so at upsetting the ecological balance, that we do not fully comprehend. We can stage a seduction, or mount a courtship, but the result is more likely to be infatuation or two illusions dancing together rather than love.

You know what's special about love? It's better than all of us. We can invite love but cannot dictate how, when, or where love expresses itself. You can choose to surrender to love or not, but in the end, love strikes like a lightning bolt, unpredictable. You can find yourself loving people you do not even like at all. Like the sun, love radiates independently of our fears and our desires.

The Importance of Discipline

Love is free, and sometimes people hate you for nothing. Love cannot be bought, sold, or traded. You cannot make someone love you, nor can you prevent it for any amount of money, when it comes to marriage it is a matter for the law, rules courts and property rights. You can buy sex partners and even marriage partners. Real love is priceless.

It is:

Sacrifice.

Philosophy.

Trust.

Respect.

Dedication.

Challenge beyond the body.

Give and take.

However, if you do not love yourself, if you're not happy with your soul, your life, your mind, you will never be able to give happiness to another. Our love will never be sustainable, it will never be sufficient. Love is honest, it is not manipulation. it is selfless, and this is the issue in society today.

I don't believe people should be hitting the lotto.

Meanwhile there's parts of the country still starving, it doesn't make sense. The things in the world and the universe will begin to change, when we begin to love each other. In the bible "John 3:16" For God so loved his world he gave his only begotten son, who so ever believes in him shall not perish but have ever lasting life." The concept of this verse to me, means he GAVE a sacrifice which is the epitome of love. Heaven and hell is on earth and you reap what you sow.

Allow me to elaborate. When you hear the word love, what is the first thing that comes to mind? Images of holding hands, softly spoken words and tender moments wrapped in intimacy and comfort. These are all fine and good. However, there are so many more levels to love that it will take a deeper knowledge and intellect to understand this. There are channels within the mind and heart that a person can tap into. This obtains something far more valuable than mere affection. I will educate you on these levels, and give you a clearer perspective on why it is with this knowledge you are able to formulate a connection, that can conquer and defeat anything coming against you.

Most people think of the first connection to love as being physical. Becoming physically attracted to your partner and having the desire to be intimate with them. But if this is necessary, then how would you explain when two people clearly show no attraction for the other, are mortal enemies even. But when forced into a traumatic situation, or a circumstance that brings these two people together beyond their control, they begin to see things in each other they never would have taken the time to notice, had the opportunity not presented itself. Very often people are confused at the evidence of seeing an obviously beautiful woman or man, with someone that is the complete opposite in physical appearance. What does he or she see in them? This is a perfect example of the first level we will speak on. And that is the spiritual level.

The Spiritual Love

The spiritual love is the first level in which a true connection is formed. This goes beyond the visual and physical stimulation that normally propels a person into desiring a connection with someone. This level correlates within the soul. When two souls touch each other, there is an intergalactic reaction that goes far deeper than can be reached with mere intimacy or affection. When souls are connected on a spiritual level the communication goes even beyond the heart. Let me explain what that means for you.

If a true connection of this sort is established, then it is not something that can be broken. Many people believe that you can just walk away, or someone doesn't really love you, and you are free to love someone else. However, with a spiritual love you are bound together with a soul clasping unity. Even if one were to walk away, the other would find their way back, or they would be brought back together beyond even their own understanding.

This is why so many individuals are ridiculed on why they would continue a relationship with someone, if they're always fighting, breaking up then getting back together again. It appears as if these two individuals are never in sync. But it goes beyond the comprehension of what is considered a normal relationship.

Now let me make this clear. I am not referring to people who are obviously in a bad partnership with someone, in which one person does not love you, and the other is giving all of themselves, but receiving nothing in return. Yet they remain with the person and constantly go back to someone who does not reciprocate their love. That is not a spiritual love. That is what's called dependency admiration. Because it is not real love. The soul can only truly love someone that recognizes and is a receptor to the connection it enfolds.

There is no such thing as "I love him, but he doesn't love me back." If he or she does not love you and touches you on that spiritual soul level, then it was never truly love in the first place. You were in a relationship with someone you greatly admired and became dependent on that person in a way that made you believe it was love. But a true spiritual love will always be reciprocated. It cannot be broken, no matter where you are in the world away from each other. It is an abiding love that weathers all matter of storms and turbulence in your life. It will be shared by both of you, and both partners will always feel it.

A spiritual love is never a one-sided thing. It is not based on the appearance of someone, or the possessions they have. This level of connection will make you love someone you never would have imagined possible. And they will love you in return so fiercely, that even if you were to pass away, that person may engage with someone else, but they will always be connected to the one that touched their soul.

The next level of connection we will speak on is of a more intellectual bond.

The Telepathic Love

This level that I am going to speak on cannot be obtained without the spiritual bond. The spiritual touching of souls is what opens the door to a deeper avenue within your mind. A level that many people have not, or do not know how to tap into.

Telepathy is widely known as a myth that is often described as being a super power found in a comic book. It is another form of communication used solely within the mind to connect with another individual. It is believed this is not something people can actually do. Let me inform you, that is far from the truth.

The telepathic level of love is a mind changing experience. Once you have reached this level with your partner, you two are in another category of existence. You are able to communicate with the one you love on a psychological connection that is above normal understanding. You often hear of couples finishing each other's sentences, or somehow knowing what the other needs before they need it. Well a telepathic love connection goes even further than that. You can feel each other's pain. You know when the other person needs you or is calling for you. Your body responds to their call. Their request. Your mind is connected with them in a way that defies logic. If they are away from you, you can feel them as if they are right next to you. And they will feel you. They know what you require before you ask it, because they are with you inside the deepest parts of your existence.

For some, the telepathic level is too strong a connection. Many fear this level of love because it requires total relinquishing of your control to someone else. Absolute trust is needed, and that is why the spiritual bond must first be formed. You could never reach this level unless the soul recognizes its other half. This is how you know and understand what is real love. True connection. Once you have reached this second level of love, where your mind and spirit have been opened, everything else becomes irrelevant and insignificant.

The last level that I will speak on is the final stage of completion. Where you and your partner have sealed the circle of connection.

The Blood Bond Love

The blood bond is connected directly to the heart. Now it is believed that the heart should be the first surrendered when speaking of love. But this is inaccurate. The heart is actually the very last. How is this possible you wonder? Many people believe you love someone and that their heart is feeling all this emotion and it is where everything begins and ends. In the bible, it clearly states that the heart is the deceiver (Jeremiah 17:9) You are deceived into believing what you think you should feel. But it is not the heart that surrenders first. The heart cannot truly give itself unless the spirit and mind are in connection with it. The heart is not the one that leads. It is the heart that follows.

The blood bond is formed when the spirit has touched, and the mind has connected. It then translates into a blood bond of the purest unity known to man. once the heart has been awakened, and that is what this truly is, an awakening of the heart. Once it has been awakened there is nothing that can break you, nothing that can defeat you.

You are literally invincible. Disappointments will come, and they will seem unimportant to you.

Challenges will appear, and you will combat them as if you are powered by an unseen force. Both of you will have reached a stage where your levels of connection have transcended the mundane, and all else becomes obsolete. Arguments won't matter, and disagreements are like puffs of smoke that quickly dissimilate within the air. This is how you hear of individuals that have lasted for twenty, thirty, even forty years or more in relationships. I don't speak of the ones that are just there for show. I refer to those that are a living testimony of how love over powers everything that may be coming your way.

With these levels of love, you have reached a point in your relationship that no one can come in between, or decipher. You can achieve anything together and overcome any obstacle. So in essence, yes, with this love, you are invincible.

CHAPTER 9 – Why Discipline is required

If you can master self and mental discipline you can take on anything you desire in this world. Discipline is a concept that everyone is aware of, but few understand. The most successful people in this world practice discipline on a daily basis. It is vital to every living being and without it, the world around us would be in chaos. To be great, to be a leader, you must display restraint. Hold yourself to a high standard. Not giving into something you truly desire is a sign of strength. Making the conscious decisions in life of the "wants" and the "needs"!

Regardless of where you exert this self-restraint, it will help promote achievements in your life. Talent without discipline is like a car without any wheels. You may be able to start it when you place the key in the ignition, however, you will not move. Discipline brings stability and structure into a person's life. If there were no discipline, people would do whatever they wanted and make mistakes without putting the consideration of others first and foremost. It promotes good human behaviour to better society and makes it a more enjoyable place for everyone to live.

Think of athletics: discipline is the fundamental aspect on which sports have been created. Every player must adhere to the rules of the game. This is why umpires and referees exist. Whoever does not follow these guidelines will be penalized for violating the rules of the sport. Persons in high authority must demonstrate high levels of restraint constantly; they cannot just speak however they see fit. A smart leader knows when to hold his tongue and when to speak. Discipline helps to train a person's mind and character, building a sense of self-control and the practice of obedience.

There are two types of discipline: internal and external. Internal discipline is your self-restraint and your ability to differentiate right from wrong. External discipline is according to societal norms, such as following the law. It is not sufficient enough to possess great qualities; we need the ability to manage them. Too many people are susceptible to instant gratification. People lacking control are unable to look at the long-term effects of their actions. This further demonstrates why this is such a crucial skill to have in life.

It is probably the most crucial factor when trying to achieve a goal. It allows you to choose from different options and by following these options you can garner the success you sought out for. It additionally gives you the authority to overcome any obstacles that come your way. This ability can be developed or strengthened at any given time if you put your mind to it. Make promises and make sure you deliver. Make the genuine effort to align your actions and behaviours with your thoughts. Exercise; get your mind and body into shape. Resist the urge to give into negative behaviours, instead focus on all of the positive attributes. To possess self-discipline is to be able to make the decisions, take the actions, and execute your game plan regardless of the obstacles, discomfort, or difficulties, that may come your way. Certainly, being disciplined does not mean living a limiting or a restrictive lifestyle. Nor, does not mean giving up everything you enjoy, or, to relinquish fun and relaxation. It does mean learning how to focus your mind and energies on your goals and persevere until they are accomplished.

It also means cultivating a mindset whereby you are ruled by your deliberate choices rather than by your emotions, bad habits, or the sway of others. Self-discipline allows you to reach your goals in a reasonable time frame and to live a more orderly and satisfying life. Learn what motivates you and what your bad triggers are.

You can begin by learning about yourself! Sometimes it is very difficult to fight off urges and cravings, so know the areas where your resistance is low and how to avoid those situations. If you know you can't resist cake, fries, or other temptations - stay away from them. Do not have them around to lure you in moments of weakness. Learn what motivates you and what your bad triggers are. You can begin by learning about yourself!

If you also know that putting pressure on yourself does not work for you, then set yourself up in an environment that encourages the building of self-discipline rather than one that sabotages it. Remove the temptations and surround yourself with soothing and encouraging items such as motivating slogans and pictures of what you want to achieve. Learn also what energizes and motivates you.

Your willpower can go up and down with your energy levels so play energetic music to perk you up, move around, laugh. Train yourself to enjoy what you are doing by being energized. This will make it easier to implement desirable and appropriate behaviours into your routine - which is really what self-discipline is all about. Make certain behaviours a routine.

Once you have decided what's important to you and which goals to strive for, establish a daily routine that will help you achieve them. For example, if you want to eat healthily or lose weight; resolve to eat several servings of fruits and vegetables each day and exercise for at least half an hour. Make it part of your daily routine and part of your self-discipline building. Likewise, get rid of some of your bad, self-defeating habits, whatever they may be.

They can put you in a negative frame of mind and hinder your self-discipline. A poor attitude can also be a bad habit. Practice self-denial. Learn to say no to some of your feelings, impulses and urges. Train yourself to do what you know to be right, even if you don't feel like doing it. Skip dessert some evenings. Limit your TV watching. Resist the urge to yell at someone who has irritated you. Stop and think before you act. Think about consequences. When you practice self-restraint, it helps you develop the habit of keeping other things under control. Engage in sports or activities. Sports are an excellent way to enhance self-discipline.

They train you to set goals, focus your mental and emotional energies, become physically fit, and to get along with others. Participating in sports provides a situation where you learn to work hard and strive to do your best, which in turn, teaches you to integrate the same the thought processes and disciplines into your everyday life. Learning to play a musical instrument can be another great way to practice self-discipline. The focus, repetition, and application required in learning to play an instrument is invaluable. Achieving self-discipline in any one area of your life reprograms your mind to choose what is right, rather than what is easy. Get inspiration from those you admire.

Michael Jordan has always maintained that his greatness as a basketball player came as much from his willingness to work hard at his craft, as it did his talent. It was his desire through discipline and focus that made him one of the best basketball players ever. If it worked for him, it could certainly work for the rest of us.

Visualize the rewards. There is nothing more gratifying than accomplishing your goals. Practice the technique that high achievers and top athletes do. Project yourself in the future. Visualize your desired outcome. Feel how rewarding it is and the countless benefits you will enjoy. Remind yourself what it takes to get there.

To be a great and inspiring leader, you must constantly display restraint. Not giving into something you truly want is a sign of strength. Making the right decisions in life can make or break you, and this type of person tends to make the right decisions. Regardless of where you exert this self-restraint, it will help to promote achievement in your life.

"Talent without discipline is like an octopus on roller skates. There's plenty of movement, but you never know if it's going to be forward, backwards, or sideways."

The ability for an individual to have self-restraint allows them to behave in a consistently stringent and controlled manner. A lack of this ability can have disastrous results.

Do you think a company is going to tolerate a person who is consistently late to work or who procrastinates in doing their work? It is evident how these behaviors will weaken the image of a business.

"Mental toughness is many things and rather difficult to explain. Its qualities are sacrifice and self-denial. Also, most importantly, it is combined with a perfectly disciplined will that refuses to give in. It's a state of mind -- you could call it character in action." — Vince Lombardi

"Self-discipline is a form of freedom. Freedom from laziness and lethargy, freedom from the expectations and demands of others, freedom from weakness and fear — and doubt. Self-discipline allows a pitcher to feel his individuality, his inner strength, his talent. He is master of, rather than a slave to, his thoughts and emotions."

Discipline can become the bridge between goals and accomplishment.

Having self-discipline is one of the most important things you will achieve in life. It gives you the ability to maintain yourself in things and people, where others lose control. This is a trait that most individuals strive for, but very often are not able to accomplish. It takes more than patience, and much more than desire, to accrue the will power to sustain your natural temptation to give in to things that the body and mind gravitate to. It takes having a primal need to be more, and knowing the end results if you meet your goals.

Self-discipline gives you the power to stick to your decisions and follow them through, without changing your mind, and is therefore, one of the important requirements for achieving goals.

The possession of this skill enables you to persevere with your decisions and plans until you accomplish them. It also manifests as inner strength, helping you to overcome addictions, procrastination and laziness, and to follow through with whatever you do.

Having Willpower and Self-Discipline

Understanding how to strengthen Your Willpower & Self-Discipline

Comprehension is the first step in learning how to strengthen your will power and self-discipline. Realizing that it is not a luxury, or desire. But must become a primal need, that will bolster and balance your life.

Strengthen Your Willpower & Self-Discipline

Being able to move away from your natural impulses, and the lure of instant gratification, is not a simple task. However, this is how you strengthen your will power. The ability to refrain from your desires, teaches you the art of self-discipline. Using two traits can assist you in doing this:

Perseverance.

The ability not to give up, despite failure and setbacks.

self-control.

The ability to resist distractions or temptations.

You will be tested, and challenged. Life will give you many reasons to give in to your more common instincts, and satisfy that driving need to relieve your desires. However, resisting that urge, is the presence of self-control. Perseverance will give you the strength to continue to master self-control, by pursuing and constantly challenging your need to give in.

The possession of this skill leads to self-confidence and self-esteem, and consequently, to happiness and satisfaction.

On the other hand, lack of self-discipline leads to failure, loss, health and relationships' problems, obesity, and to other problems.

This skill is also useful for overcoming eating disorders, addictions, smoking, drinking and negative habits. You also need it to make yourself sit and study, exercise your body, develop new skills, and for self-improvement, spiritual growth and meditation.

Having these skills will aide you in becoming more disciplined and less impulsive. These traits can help you in life in many ways, and it is with time and diligence, you will be able to find your balance and strength with these important skills.

Why self-Discipline is Beneficial and Important

Self-discipline helps you:

Avoid acting rashly and on impulse.

Fulfill promises you make to yourself and to others.

Overcome laziness and procrastination.

Continue working on a project, even after the initial rush of enthusiasm has faded away.

Go to the gym, walk or swim, even if your mind tells you to stay at home and watch TV.

Continue working on your diet, and resisting the temptation of eating fattening foods.

Wake up early in the morning.

Overcome the habit of watching too much TV.

Start reading a book, and read it to the last page.

Meditate regularly.

Self-discipline can be maintained by knowing how to:

Fully Understand its importance in your life.

Comprehension is everything. Once you realize how important the art of discipline is to your life, you can begin to incorporate it within every aspect of your daily living. It can operate as your ally. You can use the art of self-discipline to keep you focused and in control of any situation. You can master the art of winning.

The main basis of being in control, in knowing how to self-discipline your life. If you can accomplish this, then you can achieve greatness.

The Importance of Discipline

The art of having discipline is more than just being able to say you have a strong character. Having discipline in your life is needed, because of the structure it embodies, and forces you to adhere to. It instills guidelines that your mind embraces to help outline its rhythm. Contrary to what many may believe, the mind works within its own algorithm, and needs discipline to keep it functioning smoothly.

Discipline is an essential part of our life. In fact, without discipline life, we cannot work smoothly. Parents, elders of the family, and the teachers are the first persons to introduce the sense of discipline to the children. Discipline must be learned from the early stages of life. Discipline ensures the smooth flow of life without putting hindrance to the individual's liberty. Discipline teaches us to be systematic towards achieving our goal of life. It helps us to achieve our ambitions.

When we are young, discipline shapes our lives and it determines how we will operate and function as adults, in our daily rhythm. This is why when we are taught as children to go to school, wash ourselves before bed, eat certain foods, we are being conditioned and trained to self-discipline. Unfortunately, not everyone takes to early training of the conditioning of the mind. It takes a certain type of individual to break away from the crowd, and follow the traits we are taught from our youth.

A Nation cannot progress without the law-abiding disciplined citizens. This helps to build up the nation with the proper co-operations and unity. In this case, a nation can be saved from neighbor's opportunistic attitudes. Strength of a nation lies in discipline.

Order within a community, helps to enrich the lives of our young people. This is why discipline taught at a young age is crucial. It shapes not only our nation, but builds the minds of those that will lead our nation after us. If we practiced more self-discipline in our lives, and passed it down to our heirs, there would be far less impulsive and violent acts that exhibit a lack of self-control and will power.

His holiness, Dalai Lama, writes, "Self-discipline, although difficult, while combating negative emotions, should be a defensive measure. At least we will be able to prevent the advent of negative conduct dominated by negative emotion. Once we develop this, by familiarizing ourselves with it, along with mindfulness and conscientiousness, eventually that pattern and way of life, will become a part of our own life."

Self-discipline is an integral part of our lives. This is why we strive for it, and work hard to build its strength to the point of invincibility. Once you have adapted an armor of discipline, there is nothing that can distract you or deter you from your goals. It is one of the reasons why discipline is the very first trait that temptation aims to make us get rid of.

If we do not have discipline in our lives, it leaves a void of endless contradictions that replaces it. The addiction to become like everyone else takes precedence, over self-preservation. You are drawn to those things that are popular, and widely accepted. It becomes undesirable to follow your own path, or refrain from choosing to give in to your desires. You become what everyone else has resulted to. A lack of self-control and purpose.

Without discipline there is no way we can control our mind or our senses.

Know yourself and your mind. If you can control the mind, the body will follow.

In our spiritual life discipline is most essential. The spiritual activity needs systemic actions with strict discipline in life. To lead a spiritual life, a constant alertness over the mind is needed.

Certain practices insulate you, yet retain your sensitivity at the same time. This needs training and education. We all have ten fingers and though everyone has the ability, only a few can play the guitar.

Only those few who have learned how to play the guitar or the flute or the trombone can play it.

We each have a uniqueness that makes us individuals. Having self-discipline helps to shape and tailor our gifts and personalize as our own.

There is no pathway we are given, that will come without roadblocks. Discipline teaches you the art of control. It gives you the strength to overcome the challenges you will face, and still remain focused. It allows you to be all that you were created to become, and achieve the highest level of success.

Discipline works everywhere. It controls our morals and even our religion. There is no sphere in heaven and earth where discipline does not dominate.

Chapter 10 – Freedom

Freedom is a beautiful thing, however when we refer to bondage, we are all bound. Whether that be financially, physically, mentally, spiritually. Financially, we always be bound. We can't cheat our taxes. We cannot get out of paying bills. But with everything else you have complete control over. In America we have our Amendments, our Freedoms and our Rights. However, TRUE Freedom is when you are able to do things without the fear of judgment, resentment and being labeled.

Many people do not accomplish some of their goals and dreams, because they are slaves to their minds. Slaves to other people's thoughts and desires. Rosa Parks, who did not give up her seat on the bus on December 1st 1955, said; "You must never be fearful about what you are doing when it is right."

Freedom is a funny thing; there are more privileges for white Americans, than there are for Black Americans. It is wrong, but I believe privileges are irrelevant. You create your own, just like you create your own luck.

Do not allow people to dictate your future. Work hard in every aspect, mind body and soul. Free yourself from bad toxins and energies ahead for you. Those things will bring you down and stop you from accomplishing whatever you were willing to accomplish. Most successful people, most alpha males and females, most businesswomen and men, most authors, entrepreneurs, all had someone or some people that told them:

- "No, that will never work"

- "Don't do that, it's too risky"

For example, Michael Jackson (RIP) had a track called "Remember the Time" in 1992. Now he also had a video to the song, which displayed for the first time on TV, a Black Egyptian King (portrayed by Eddie Murphy), it was also directed by Michael himself who also funded most of the video because the music company were not willing to support his vision. This just shows you must take a leap of faith and believe you'll make it work. When you make it work, you'll have nothing to show those doubters but pure success.

It takes a lot of guts and drive to stand for what you believe in, and to accomplish what you desire. You will experience adversity, doubters, judgers, bad energy, envy etc. Work around those things. Do not allow the distractions to make you lose focus on goals or tasks you have in place for yourself. When I was writing my book, there were so many distractions. I was Finalizing chapters, naming them and so on.

It was mentally, physically and spiritually draining. I had friends whom were texting and calling about going out to parties. Now even though I love to dance and am very outgoing, I denied them. I set a goal for myself. A deadline, and would not allow anything or anyone to set things back. I was adamant about finishing and getting it complete and out in a timely fashion. What you need to put in your mind is you are not a slave to these things. You do not need the party/club. The party/club needs You.

Priority versus wants, non-priorities. These mundane things will always be there. Your goals and the things you want, and need will not. You may drag them out. You may procrastinate with them. However, that can be detrimental to where you crave to be. What's stopping you from reaching your goal? Is it people? Things people have you think you can obtain as well? Things you witness on television? Things people tell you, because they cannot achieve what you are about? What's stopping you? I'll tell you. It's You. You are stopping yourself. Free your mind, body and soul of all those bad energies and you will always be free.

Why having intellectual freedom matters

Many have heard of the term, freedom of speech. But do you truly understand the real meaning behind the words? Or why it was included in the U.S. constitution? This is a term that is often misconstrued as having the right to say whatever we feel, yet also having the freedom from any consequences behind that free speech. This is not the case. In this section I will break down the true nature of what intellectual freedom means, and why it should matter to you.

Freedom of speech gives you the right to speak freely, being able to write or verbalize your opinion, as is your right. Ever since it was passed by law into the first amendment, along with the bill of rights, on September 25, 1789, and was adopted into the constitution on December 15, 1791. This has been the way of the American people. However, many individuals take this to mean the freedom and privilege to say and speak slanderous and often threatening verbiage to the public, without risk of punishment. And this is where the entire meaning of freedom of speech has been misunderstood.

Intellectual freedom gives you the right to verbalize your thoughts, and opinions, and share these opinions with the world. However, understand that there is a consequence to everything that you do. Freedom does not mean without threat of action to a direct injustice. Everything has a price. If you choose to verbalize your thoughts, realize that even though you are more than free to do so, there will be some sort of diverse action against you. It could be positive, or negative. But expect to receive feedback, and response.

For example, if you are a well-known journalist, and have written stories that were very popular and loved by the public. You may be inclined to step outside your box and decide to talk about something controversial. Perhaps get something off of your chest. Journalists are respected reporters, highly sought after for their work. So anything they write, more than likely will be seen by everyone. So as a journalist, you decide to start writing about sex trafficking, or conspiracy theories in high corporate places. This is a very sensitive area, and many individuals have lost their careers and even their lives, over the things they have written and spoken about. Yes, they were all able to express themselves freely. However, the price is often too high for the moment of freedom you are given.

Intellectual freedom can be used in many good ways. To encourage others that speaking out on positivity and empowerment is always a needed factor. There are many people talking on the ravages of society, and what is going on in our world today. But not enough of those that are willing to stand up and actually impact the change to make it happen.

Freedom of speech doesn't have to be a grand statement all the time. Sometimes it's a matter of just making an effort to write daily on your own blog, and spread something positive. Creating a sense of strength and a power movement, always begins with you.

So what exactly should an individual do to express themselves? How can you use intellectual freedom to your advantage, while still protecting yourself and those around you? By using wisdom, knowledge, and positivity. Never spread a message of hate, and dissension. All this will do in turn is create a more ensuing problem for yourself. One that you may not be able to pull yourself out of. Knowing how to use wisdom with your right to express your intellectual freedom, will go a long way in helping you to avoid unnecessary problems.

You can do this by starting out slowly. If you don't already have a public platform, create one for yourself. Social media is the best and easiest way for anyone to freely express themselves in today's world, and it doesn't take much education to do this. In today's growing world of technology, children as young as four years old, are using social media to gain access to what was before impossible to occupy, if you weren't a celebrity. Now, anyone can create a blog, webpage, Facebook, Instagram, snapchat, or a number of other sites where you can talk or display about anything you feel like.

However, as I mentioned before, there are limitations, even on free social media giants as these. You still must be careful what you say and display, as the consequences will often be a shut down of your page, and loss of all your followers that you may have gained.

Even on places like social media, your words and actions are carefully being monitored and observed. Yes, you have the freedom to say what you want. However, you can rest assured swift action will be taken to prevent you from saying anything further, such as the complete removal of your page. If you are considered a threat, you may not even be able to create a new one.

Social media is a great tool to use to begin utilizing your intellectual freedom, however you must understand exactly how to do this the right way. There are many programs out there today, that help with social media growth. But for today, we will talk about the basics of beginning with expressing your rights to speak. And how you can engage in this on your own.

First, you will need to figure out what exactly is it that you want to say. What message do you want to deliver to the public, and are you prepared to back up the information you are displaying? If you are stepping out into a professional area, do you have knowledge on the topic you're giving details on? Do you have proof or testimonials to give yourself credibility with the public?

Perhaps you don't want to start out as a full professional in your area. Maybe you want to begin small, and set up a personal page. And just build your followers from there. This is also something you can do, if you are limited in resources and time. You can start with the basics, depending on whatever it is you specialize in. Let's say you are a model, or an author, or a mechanic, or perhaps just aspiring to be one, or something else. Maybe you're none of those, and you just want to share your thoughts. Even with no profession, you still need a theme to adapt, if you want to be taken seriously. No matter what you do, people will judge you based on what you display and say.

You always have a choice. What you choose to do is crucial in developing the type of audience you will receive to your message. How you start out will determine the flow of things, so be careful how you begin your platform. Yes, people are always able to change down the road, or even create a whole new page and start over if possible. However, how you start will always leave you with a reputation you must live with. And that reputation will always follow you.

Take your time and develop yourself. Freedom of speech comes with a certain responsibility, and whatever you say can and will be held against you in a court of law. You must be careful of what you say, and how you say it. So in essence, is it really freedom of speech? Yes, but with consequences attached to it.

Intellectual freedom can be used to provide encouragement and fulfillment of purpose, if conducted the right way. Starting slowly, and building your message helps to create a more knowledgeable base you can use to keep you successful.

Everyone has a voice, and the opportunity to express their rights. But once you know how to use wisdom in combination with this, your influence will grow as well as your followers. People will gravitate around you to hear the message they value and appreciate.

So how do you cultivate this, without causing friction and spreading dissension? By empowering and showing an example of leadership. Everyone wants to be a master at something, but not everyone knows how to teach and educate. The best way to do this, is by learning from the best. Growing your own knowledge base and fortifying yourself against self-doubt and procrastination.

Having a public platform can be a wonderful and rewarding way to use your intellectual freedom to your advantage. But you must take the time and understand the limits of this freedom. And be aware that if you are in the public eye, your words, and actions will always be scrutinized.

You can prevent most of the mishaps from social media disasters from occurring, by doing your homework. Equipping yourself with the do's and don'ts of social media, and even public speaking. Many individuals never take the time to think through a strategy or plan of action, for public speaking, or even writing in a public blog. Therefore, you see the evidence of uninteresting social media posts, and people using their platform to simply bash the opposite sex. Many are often too fearful to talk about anything of relevance. Because it requires too much time and effort to educate themselves on the subject at hand.

If there were more individuals that truly understood the real concept of intellectual freedom, we would have less mainstream media delivering what they believe everyone wants to see and read. Violence, and human tragedy.

This is a society that cultivates dependency, encourages victimhood and discourages change that emerges from outside its boundaries and ideological parameters. Modern democratic society has the potential to be an information society, precisely because it is founded on intellectual freedom. Always do your research.

The beauty of Self-Knowledge and Mastery of the Self

Spiritual growth is impossible without self-knowledge. Man should know his own self and recognize that which leadeth unto loftiness or lowliness, glory or abasement, wealth or poverty.

To know your self-worth, is another form of freedom. The human mind is a very complex, but exquisitely made part of the human anatomy. We develop, we grow, and we connect with others, as we were designed to. This is a form of freedom that we are given that enables us to live our lives as unparalleled, and a highly diverse species.

We can detach from the things of this world. In many instances we are reminded that this physical life is only temporary, and that its pleasures are as nothing in comparison with the joys of the spirit:

We are created to be above and lead. To dominate other species as the primary leaders placed here on earth. The freedom we are given to do this, is not used to the full capacity it should be. By separating your mind from the ravages of the mass media, and temptations of the world, you are creating a peace and freedom that comes with knowledge of self.

By detachment, it is not meant however, that we should force ourselves to endure excessive deprivations. On the contrary, it is perfectly acceptable to enjoy the things of this world, as long as we remember to nurture our spirits. Our flesh is temporary, but spiritual freedom is forever.

Chapter 11 – Adapt or Perish

Evolution is inevitable, well physically it is. But how can your mind and soul reciprocate, when you are one dimensional? You are limiting yourself to becoming one way, or one thing.

Just as it is the same with the carnivorous felines in the jungle, they adapt or they perish. Because only the strong survive. The strong only know how to survive. Their prime incentive is hunger, no matter the demographics or situation. One must transform and dominate. The true character of an individual is not measured when he/she is at their highest. It's measured when he/she is at their complete lowest.

Put life into your work, into your pleasures, into yourself. Quit doing things half headed, halfheartedly. Take immense interest in what you are doing, saying and thinking. No man or woman amounted to anything, unless he/she put life into tasks of every day, the acts or the thoughts. Once you begin to say 'I' or 'best', in your sentences or thoughts, that is what you become. 'I' am alive, 'I' am the 'best'. Every cell in your body has been eavesdropping on your thoughts, and now your body and spirit are reacting to it. There is nothing in this world that is too good for you, or you don't deserve. Not a thing. Not anyone. In any situation, or in any environment, you find yourself within, you must learn to adapt and grow.

In order to conquer the things that has challenged you or tested your endurance. If you do not learn to adjust quickly to circumstances that will constantly try and assess your ability to withstand, you will perish. This goes a lot further than just in your professional life, and goals. If you do not conquer every aspect of resistance that has held you back, even things within your childhood, they will become like weeds, growing and assimilating within your subconscious.

I'm going to break this down for you in sections, by giving you a clear picture as to why this substantiates many beliefs regarding success and failure. Why it all borders down to the survival of the fittest, and the real meaning behind the saying: only the strong survive.

In the law of the jungle it is quite clear, that if you are not strong you cannot lead. And if you are not fast and cunning, you will not live. A simple equation of the food chain. Whoever is at the top, gets fed the most. And very rarely does the one at the top get eaten, or loses. He's at the top of the food chain, which means he has proven he is the strongest among the animals. However, pay very close attention to what I'm about to say, because this is why so many people often perish. Sometimes even the strong.

Just because you are at the top of the food chain means absolutely nothing, if you have not adapted to your current environment. Plainly speaking, if you are a lion with the mindset of lamb, you will very quickly lose your newly found position at the top. And someone more cunning than you will have learned to better adapt to a situation of challenge.

Understand that you can be strong physically, yet still too weak to withstand a position of power. Or you can be above average intellectually, but would not be able to hold a candle when faced with brute strength. Learning to adapt to your environment places you in an area of control, regardless of whatever attribute you may lack. If you know how to grow and can learn to interchange with whatever obstacles you are faced with, you will remain at the top.   In many instances anyone can learn to become a strong leader. However, it is not only about being physically capable, although that is paramount in commanding a powerful presence. Adapting also means to learn all aspects of what surrounds you. To be able to be comfortable in an environment that is completely out of the norm for you. To not only understand it, but use it to your own advantage and benefits.

Assess your situation.

Determine what you will need in order to survive the new surroundings. Are you in a jungle? Then you will need not only strength, but also great observation skills. You must constantly watch your back in the jungle. Dissect your enemies and their strategies. But you must also be careful of those you keep close to you, as in the jungle someone is also trying to be king.

Have you received a promotion in a career you've been working years to achieve? Then you will need your intellect as well as endurance abilities to continue to maintain that position. Your intellect is what helped you to get the promotion in the first place. Now your endurance will help you keep it. Sometimes this requires longevity in stamina, your ability to work longer hours than you're used to. Being able to undertake projects that are beyond your expertise. It will also take a lot of patience, as you will not understand many things at first. And everything will appear overwhelming in the beginning. You will be challenged and broken down by your oppressors.

Those that want what you currently possess, or simply need you removed because you are a threat to their existence. Either way, if you have not assessed your situation properly, you will be unprepared to adapt to your new environment. The opposition will defeat you, and you will lose everything.

Be silent.

When you are in a new situation, or surroundings, and you are still learning your way around, do not be so quick to share your findings. You still are not certain who are your friends and who are your enemies. Beware of those that are openly sublime and generous in your presence, but secretly are watching you for weaknesses. You will not know who are your true allies until you have weeded out the hidden thorns. I know you're thinking this sounds drastic and harsh. But keep in mind, there is always someone who wants to take your place. You can either learn to adapt and counteract anything coming at you. Or, you can perish pathetically, while watching someone else do what you couldn't.

Take no prisoners.

In the art of war, when in battle there is a saying regarding taking no prisoners. It's often used as a term to give the image of a conquered victory. But this description is only half accurate. When you are faced with challenges, and have encountered those that are obvious enemies, people that have drawn a line and made you aware of their intention to take whatever it is that belongs to you, you would be foolish to hesitate in immediately handling this problem.

For example, let's say you are a construction worker, and have been on the job for years. You're well liked and often go after work for drinks with your friends. But now, you've recently received the job as head foreman of the whole project. A job all of your friends would give their left arm to have. Suddenly none of them wants to hang with you anymore. And those that do, are now overly nice to you, more than they were before. One day on the job, one of your so-called friends decides to challenge your new authority. Making jokes about you, telling everyone that you're not capable of handling such a responsibility, you can't even handle your wife.

Now, in a situation like this, it's obvious that not only are you being challenged about your ability to lead, your being questioned about your own manhood. This of course will have several results. Either you will garner such rage and immediately beat the man down, showing your physical prowess over him. Or you will begin to engage in a back and forth shouting and shoving match, which will only prove how weak you really are. In both scenarios, you lose. The oppressor will have gained the results he was hoping for. Which was to bait you in front of everyone, show that you have no self-control, and possibly cause you the new promotion you just recently gained.

This is where assessing the situation, and being silent comes in handy. If you observed your environment accurately, you would already have seen this snake before he slithered to make his move. And when you are silent and still, the snake does not know what move to make.

He's watching you, but you are also watching him. In this challenge, your enemy has made his move, and your job is clear. You do not react to the insults of the challenge. You are the foreman. You are the leader.

If one of your crew has been subordinate in anyway, he should immediately be fired. Handle it in a professional way, that leaves no question of your authority. This will send a very clear message to those around you. You are not there to be their friends. On the job you are the boss. The top of the food chain. If they cannot accept that, they will be removed. It doesn't matter the history, or how many drinks you all shared together. Take no prisoners. If you exact your leadership with no hesitancy, your authority will be respected in your new surroundings.

The last thing we will go over is acceptance.

After you have assessed, and learned to become silent as you observed all around you, and understood the meaning behind taking no prisoners, you must also be ready to accept that you will be hated. Especially if you are accustomed to being admired, and usually a very popular person. Throw all of that away. And I'm not just referring to promotions. Keep in mind this all applies in life to everything. In any place or opportunity, you come to, you will have to adapt to it. You will need to learn how to adjust outside of your comfort zone, if you are ever going to grow. These are just key things that will help you to better grasp the foundation of what you need to succeed at it.

Acceptance is the hardest thing to achieve when adapting to a new element of change. You can acquire all the other things I've spoken about. But if you cannot accept that you will be hated, you will still fail. Understand why the lion, who is king of the jungle, is often alone. He has his lionesses, but very rare are there other grown male lions, in the same pride, if one is already king. Unless they are trying to overthrow the current one. The lion king has to constantly defend his pride against invaders. Even his own sons will challenge him when they come of age. This is why the grown male lions must leave the pride when they come of age, so they can build their own. The lion king stands alone. This is the same for people who are in positions of power, or even those who are up and coming.

When you have a talent, and you stand out over others, you will be challenged for that gift, and if you are victorious, you will be hated. There will be those that will smile and pretend they are with you. But we've already gone over how snakes operate. It is true that it can be very lonely at the top of the food chain. Because you were the strongest, the most cunning, and patient enough to get there. And it will be even more challenging to see longtime friends walk away from you.

The Importance of Discipline

Peers will begin to judge you. Create accusations about you, and try to make you look and feel like trash. It will be hard to withstand this. But with much success comes great intellect. And you must have the wisdom to know that in order to remain at the top, there will be a few things you will have to accept and let go. Habits that you must walk away from, and people that you will need to remove from your life. These are all key factors you will need in learning to adapt to any environment in which you encounter. Once you have understood and controlled the true concept of this, the top of the chain, as a leader, is where you will always remain.

Chapter 12 – Knowledge vs Understanding

We are all smart. Everyone is incredibly knowledgeable about something. However, we are not all intelligent. Where there are a few that are knowledgeable about a little of everything. Education does not equate to intelligence. Plenty of people know of you, but how many actually understand you? If knowledge is power, what is understanding? Control?

When we go to school, we are taught of the 'how's' but not of the 'why's'. Having the information in front of you is one thing. Having the comprehension and the understanding is a completely different thing.

Knowledge refers to information or awareness gained through experience or education. Understanding refers to knowing or realizing the intended meaning or cause of something. For example, you may count the names of the presidents of the US. But it's because of your understanding that the US. Is a country that elects its president every four years, and that some presidents have served two consecutive terms. Which is equate to eight years.

If you as a student understand the concept explained by your teacher, but have gained no knowledge, you will get nowhere. Knowledge without understanding is merely an example of a good memory. How much knowledge do you understand on a deeper level?

For example, we may all know that placing a raw egg into boiling water will cook the egg. But we don't necessarily understand the process that effects the protein within the egg. But a specialist who studies the process will not only learn how, but also understand why.

When I was younger, I was told to eat my broccoli and oatmeal, and others. I would ask, why? My parents would say: 'Callate', or 'Ferme la bouche', which in Spanish and French means: 'Shut up' or 'shut your mouth and just do it'.

As I became older, I learned why water is essential. And why fruits and vegetables are essential to my body, mind and health. In essence, understanding is a deep process with great benefits. Whereas simple book knowledge, note learning, or mnemonic style information occupies a very shallow level of the mind, and so gives minimal benefits.

It is only when someone has learned it well enough to apply it in the moment, they can fully understand and grow from the knowledge. Knowledge ultimately being the collection of past events, and second-hand knowledge obtained elsewhere. In the present moment there is simply understanding and the opening towards serenity and happiness.

In this segment, I will break down the differences between the two categories, and how it is imperative that you identify, and gain comprehension, as to why this is beneficial to you.

Knowledge is what we use to obtain power. To achieve certain statuses in life, and move from levels that were not enough to gain the importance of recognition, we all hope to procure. Having knowledge of something gets you into places that were before closed to you. Promotions, highly coveted careers, political offices, and can even help you to gain the trust of people that surround and speak to you.

Having knowledge of something, especially when it is clear you have an exceeding amount of it in a particular field or subject, places you in a position of honor in most people's eyes. You are considered an expert in your mode of specialty, and are looked upon with favor and reverence. As I stated earlier, many people are smart. But not everyone possesses the intellect to converse on a subject that may take years of education to obtain the knowledge in.

This advantage creates certain benefits for you as an individual. If you are knowledgeable in an area that people need or use, you can command certain privileges that others cannot. Starting your own business, or becoming a speaker and educating those on the things you have learned. Demanding a higher salary from your job because of the more information you are able to give to your employer.

There are so many that have no idea how having more knowledge can elevate you in life. You don't have to be intellectual of everything. There is something that everyone is blessed with and can do. A talent that God has given to everyone. If you were to tap into the gift that you possess, then gaining information on your particular talent would only increase what you already have.

I don't care if there are hundreds of people that are good doctors. If that is your goal, then gain the education you need and be the best doctor in your field. If you want to dance and have been told that dancers are a dime a dozen, continue anyway, and capitalize on what you have inside of you. Gaining the wisdom you require to expound on something you're naturally good at, can only take you to the top.

Allow me to explain further how this can assist you in everything you do.

I'm going to give you an example of a giraffe and a turtle. Two completely different animals, at two very different levels. The turtle crawls along the ground at a ridiculously slow pace, in which it sometimes appears that he's not even moving. He is vulnerable to all types of attacks, and the only thing that saves him is his shell. The moment there is danger he hides in this shell and remains there until it's safe to emerge again. Hiding and crawling. This is all the turtle knows.

Now you have the giraffe. A tall statuesque creature that can see even above the trees at times. He can run at a gallop when there is danger, and he can graze among the pastures because he can travel faster. He is freer than the turtle, but they both live in the jungle.

Now imagine for a moment, that the turtle and the giraffe were friends. Two totally opposite animals, just hanging out together. And the giraffe says to the turtle one day: "I think I want to go beyond the jungle. I see waters over there that look deeper than the ones we drink at. I see fields that are safer to run in, and it looks more peaceful over there. Come with me, turtle. Let's try it and see."

But the little turtle cannot see what the giraffe is witnessing. Remember, his life is on the ground. He crawls. So he looks at the giraffe and says: "Are you crazy? We can't risk all the dangers that will come to us if we move. There are snakes and people that will step on us. Poison that can get on our skin. No, it's safer to remain exactly where we are."

Here you have two animals that see two very different viewpoints. The turtle only has knowledge of what is before him. And sees nothing at his level to prompt him to want to learn more. But the giraffe has a higher advantage. He can see things other animals cannot. He has talents that other creatures wish they had. But if the giraffe listens to the turtle, and decides to remain where he is out of fear, he will never be able to expound on the knowledge he could gain. Just by taking that step to learn more.

Knowledge is needed in order for you to gain the advantage in life. Do not allow people or circumstances to dictate what you can and cannot achieve. Empower yourself. Inform yourself. Educate yourself. Equip yourself to become greater than you already are. Once you do that, there is no challenge you will not be able to face.

Now let's switch gears a moment and talk about understanding. It is crucial that with having knowledge, you also gain the understanding you need to keep and secure that intellect.

There is no way you can have wisdom of something, yet have no comprehension of the information you possess. If that is the case, then you were never knowledgeable in the first place.

For example. If you were to approach a teacher who has education in the field of mental health and therapy, and started asking them in depth questions regarding schizophrenia and the effects of it, you would want answers. You would expect the teacher to not only be knowledgeable in this area, you would fully expect them to understand what it is you are talking about.

However, a teacher can obtain a job and a get a degree in any field, and still not truly have an understanding of what it is they have learned.

Having understanding breaks down the mechanics of the information you have been given. It is not enough to just gain the knowledge. You have to comprehend the meaning behind what it is you have obtained.

Again, this goes back to the giraffe and the turtle. If the giraffe has the knowledge that there are other things out there that can better him, and get him further than the jungle, he must also understand why the turtle cannot go with him. The turtle will never be able to see what he can see, and do what he can do. If the giraffe fully understands this, then he will know that taking advice from a turtle who is nowhere near his level, is not the wisest thing to do.

Understanding is elemental in everything that you have. If you obtain knowledge without having the understanding of what you recently achieved, it is no better than claiming a fancy luxurious mansion, and then gaining no access to it.

If you place these two key factors hand in hand with each other, then you become unstoppable. You can reach the heights that you've been dreaming of, and monopolize your growth in areas that were before closed to you.

Knowledge is power. But having the understanding that comes with it, will help you to keep and maintain the power you have accomplished. You will be able to overstep your peers, because you took the time and the extra effort to become more. To see more. To know more. And no one will be able to take that away from you. Once you have this, and compound it with your talents, the levels in life that you will reach will exceed even your own expectations.

They say that 'knowledge is power' and while this is technically meant more metaphorically than literally it is nevertheless true in a very direct way.

There's a film called 'Three Days of the Condor', and in it a man hired by the CIA is tasked with reading as many books as possible of all genres in order to search them for hidden codes and messages that could be relayed by spies within the country. Of course, the main purpose of this task is for him to find evidence of enemies communicating state secrets, but there is a side effect from reading so much – he becomes incredibly knowledgeable.

This surplus of knowledge gives him the ability to work out that members of the CIA are in fact trying to kill him. Fortunately, his new skills include tapping phones, running evasive patterns when being fired at, performing forensic science and picking locks. It's a fictional story of course, but it nevertheless illustrates just how it is possible to become almost a superhero through knowledge alone.

Here we will look at why knowledge is so powerful and at how you can go about using it in order to become a better version of yourself.

Become the Best at Whatever You Do

The first kind of knowledge you should seek to accumulate is knowledge that relates to your lifestyle and to what you do. A mechanic for instance should make it their business to learn absolutely everything they can about vehicles and about mechanical engineering. This way they will then be able to repair cars better than anyone else and they will be likely to get the most business and the best business.

Excel for Innovation

True greatness and innovation in a field is said to come about in two ways. One way is by being a complete novice in your field – which means that your ideas and your concepts are completely original and unhindered by thought that has gone before you. The other way is by being a complete expert and by knowing absolutely everything there is to know on a subject. This then in theory means that you are able to weigh up all of the information you have evenly, and to come up with the best solution bearing that in mind. Having no knowledge on a subject greatly limits what you are capable of achieving and has other problems – for instance you can unwittingly plagiarize if you aren't aware of what's come before you. Thus to be a true innovator – to improve the world around you and to go down in history – you need knowledge.

Become knowledgeable for Social Reasons

As we discussed in a previous chapter, having knowledge can help you gain stature within social media platforms. It can give you the confidence you need to become an expert in your field of topic. This is one of the greatest reasons to obtain knowledge to further your career and social media influence.

At the same time a lack of knowledge can be highly embarrassing if you are caught out there. For instance, if everyone is talking about something that's happening in the news, or if everyone is discussing a historical event; and in either situation you don't know what they are talking about and are unable to contribute, then this will often make you feel out of the loop or even unintelligent and you will be branded ignorant. On the other hand, having something interesting and insightful to bring to everyone's conversation will make you seem attractive, intelligent and well read. In an interview situation this will make you more likely to get the job, while in a dating situation this is a good way to impress a potential partner – knowledge and intelligence are very attractive traits.

To Adapt to Situations

If you have a lot of knowledge, then you will be able to adapt to any situation and will never be caught unaware. Locked out of your home? Then the ability to pick locks could come in handy. Car won't start? Then if you can jump start it yourself you will be laughing. No software for what you need to do? Well then why not program your own. Someone choking? Then hopefully you know the Heimlich maneuver. The more knowledge you have the more likely you are to be able to adapt to the situation and to help yourself and others. It will save you time, bring you satisfaction and ensure that others are impressed.

It can be used For Power

Having knowledge and information is what tells you how to manipulate the world around you. Even something seemingly 'useless' such as historical knowledge has very useable benefit (knowing the past helps you to navigate the present and future). In short, the more you know, the better you will be able to manipulate your surroundings and the more you will be free from usual restraints. Knowledge then really is power.

What is Knowledge?

First let us pay attention to the concept of Knowledge. This can be defined as the information or awareness gained through experience or education. It goes beyond the depths of understanding allowing a person to develop his faculties. Hence, one can state that Knowledge is greater than understanding. We make casual use of the word knowledge in daily conversation.

For an example when we say, 'This is correct to the best of my knowledge,' this means that as far as the individual is aware, the particular information is accurate. The facts such as timing of your favorite TV show, the names of 20th century US Presidents, top ten songs of the week, the number of the bus you catch daily to reach the office, your height, and weight, and the opening and closing of Dow Jones today, can be easily categorized as your knowledge, but they are different from understanding as they are not open to arguments.

They are facts that cannot be argued and form a knowledge base that helps you in your life. This highlights the nature of knowledge.

Difference Between Knowledge and Understanding

What is Understanding?

Now let us move on to the term Understanding. This can be defined as knowing or realizing the intended meaning or cause of something. This can also be referred to as the interpretation or view of a particular thing. For an example, we read a poem and attempt to understand what the poet is trying to say. We unravel the hidden meanings through a deep understanding. This highlights that understanding something refers to an interpretation.

Let us gain a better comprehension of this word through another example. Why was Pluto stripped of its status as a planet of our solar system, how does an AC work, or the principle of flow of electrons in a conductor can be categorized as your understanding that is open for arguments and also for probe or testing. This emphasizes that unlike knowledge that is fact based and can be presented as statements that are not open to further questioning, understanding requires longer statements, their explanation, and probably corrections when someone points out any in-congruence. We check understanding of a person when we conduct a test and not his knowledge. Now let us summarize the difference in the following manner.

Knowledge vs Understanding

What's the Difference Between Knowledge and Understanding?

Knowledge refers to information or awareness gained through experience or education. Whereas understanding refers to knowing or realizing the intended meaning or cause of something.

Chapter 13 – Evolve

How can the evolution of one species affect the evolution of another? No species exists in a vacuum; every form of life on Earth interacts over time with other organisms, as well as with its physical environment. For that reason, the evolution of one species influences the evolution of species with which it coexists by changing the natural selection pressures those species face. The classic examples of this sort of evolution, called coevolution, are predator-prey and host-parasite relationships.

One such predator-prey relationship exists between garter snakes and a species of salamander-like amphibian called a rough-skinned newt. In parts of the midwestern United States, garter snakes prey on newts, and probably have for thousands of years. In that time, over countless generations, the newts have evolved a powerful defense: a toxic chemical that they secrete through their skin. Where garter snakes are concerned, however, this defense mechanism has only been marginally successful.

Generation after generation, as the newts became more poisonous, the snakes also evolved, developing greater tolerance to the newt's toxin. The result of this coevolutionary process, played out over countless snake and newt generations, is a chemical more toxic than almost any other natural substance on Earth, and a population of snakes that are seemingly immune to the toxin's effects. What does it mean when some scientists say humans have stopped evolving? Technology and culture have protected us to a great extent from the selective pressures that drive evolution, allowing many people, especially those in developed nations who would otherwise not live to reproductive age, to pass their genes on to the next generation. In addition, human groups are no longer isolated; they travel the globe. Without genetic isolation, there is no further opportunity for speciation among humans.

On the other hand, natural selection is a function of environmental change, and our physical, biological, and cultural environments have changed tremendously. Humans face, for example, new diseases like HIV/AIDS that can greatly impact survival and reproduction. Human populations may also be undergoing evolutionary changes of which we're not yet aware. If extinction is a natural part of life on Earth, why should we care about protecting endangered species?

If the mass extinction most scientists agree we're experiencing now is allowed to continue, it will be the first time in the history of life on Earth that a single species would be responsible for such a catastrophe. And although extinction is a natural process that has occurred many times in the distant past, it's a process that would be in our best interest to avoid. The extinction of just one species can dramatically impact many others, and like all creatures, humans rely heavily on other species.

It is therefore impossible to predict how we might ultimately be affected by a mass extinction. How does evolution affect me in my daily life? We can and do experience the indirect effects of evolution nearly every day. One of the more important evolutionary concerns facing humans today is the continual evolution of antibiotic-resistance in bacteria. The successful medical battle we have waged against bacteria for the last 50 years is now an even race, according to some scientists. Similarly, the use of pesticides in agriculture has driven the evolution of resistant insects, requiring the use of harsher chemicals in greater quantity to kill them.

You were not put on this earth to remain the same. Evolution is all about growth. Mind, body and spirit. Circumstances does not make the man. It reveals him to himself. No such conditions can exist as descending into vice and its attendant sufferings, apart from vicious inclinations, or ascending into virtue and its pure happiness.

Without the continued cultivation of virtuous aspiration, and man/woman, therefore as the lord and master of thought, is the master of him/herself. The shaper and author of your environment.

At birth, the soul comes into its own. And through every step of its earthly pilgrimage, it attracts those combinations and conditions which reveal itself. Which are the reflections of its own purity and impurity. Its strength and weaknesses. Men and women do not attract that which they want, but that which they are. They do not get what they wish or pray for, but justly earn.

Wishes and prayers are gratified, when they harmonize with the thoughts and actions.

People are anxious to improve their circumstances, but are unwilling to improve themselves. They therefore remain bound. The ones who don't shrink from self-crucifying, can never fail to accomplish the object upon which his/her heart is set upon. You reap what you sow. You are in charge of all your circumstances. But it begins with self-improvement. Good thoughts and actions can never produce bad results. Bad thoughts and actions can never produce good results. Circumstances which a man or woman encounters with suffering, are the results of his/her own mental in harmony. As an individual alters their thoughts towards things and other people, things and other people will alter towards him/her.

The evidence of this is in every person, and it therefore admits of easy investigation by systematic inspection, and self-analysis.

Let a man or woman radically alter their thoughts, behaviors, perceptions, actions, and they will be astonished at the rapid transformation it will affect in the material conditions of their life. As the physically weak person can make themselves strong by proper and patient training, the man/woman with weak thoughts can make themselves strong by exercising himself/herself with right thinking.

To put away aimlessness and weakness, and to begin thinking with purpose, is to enter the ranks of the strong ones, who only recognize failure as one of the pathways to strong thinking and attainment. Those that make all conditions serve them. And whom attempt fearlessly, and accomplish mastery.

Evidence that shows We Are Still Evolving

As we grow, our bodies change. But there is more to it than just simply human cells developing and maturing. Our mind has abilities that are far beyond our comprehension. We show signs of evolution every day, as we witness miracles, and isolated cases where people are experiencing the amazing ability to endure unusual circumstances.

But not only are we still evolving, we're doing so even faster than before. In the last 10,000 years, the pace of our evolution has sped up 100 times, creating more mutations in our genes, and more natural selections from those mutations. There are several indications that show humans are continuing to evolve.

The consumption of Milk

History indicates the gene that regulated a human's ability to digest lactose shut down as they were weaned off of their mother's breast milk. But when we began domesticating cows, sheep and goats, being able to drink milk became a nutritionally advantageous quality, and people with the genetic mutation that allowed them to digest lactose were better able to propagate their genes.

A 2006 study suggests this tolerance for lactose was still developing as early as 3,000 years ago in East Africa. That genetic mutation for digesting milk is now carried by more than 95 percent of Northern European descendants.

The Loss of Our Wisdom Teeth

We have been losing our teeth since as far back as time was first recorded. However the loss of our wisdom teeth indicates an evolution of our genetic structure that we are still conducting research on.

Today, we have utensils to cut our food. Our meals are softer and easier to chew, and our jaws are much smaller as a result, which is why wisdom teeth are often impacted when they come in — there just isn't room for them. Like the appendix, wisdom teeth have become vestigial organs. One estimate says 35 percent of the population is born without wisdom teeth, and some say they will disappear altogether.

We've Become More Resistant to Diseases

Science and culture have developed multiple resources in being able to combat the well-known diseases today, that have plagued the human species in the past. But our bodies have also grown to develop a resistance to the common cold, and other more deadly infections that have before wiped out a large portion of the human population.

Our Brains Are Growing Smaller in Size

There has been speculation that our large brains make us smarter than the rest of the known world. However, our brains have actually been shrinking over the last 30,000 years. The average volume of the human brain has decreased from 1,500 cubic centimeters to 1,350 cubic centimeters, which is equivalent to a chunk the size of a tennis ball.

There are several different conclusions as to why this is: It was discovered that a group of researchers suspects our shrinking brains mean we are in fact getting dumber. Historically, brain size decreased as societies became larger and more complex, suggesting that the safety net of modern society negated the correlation between intelligence and survival. But in another documentary, researchers have a theory that says our brains are shrinking not because we're getting dumber, but because smaller brains are more efficient. This theory suggests that, as they shrink, our brains are being rewired to work faster but take up less room. There's also a theory that smaller brains are an evolutionary advantage because they make us less aggressive beings, allowing us to work together to solve problems, rather than tear each other to shreds.

The increased Colorization of Our Eyes

History has shown that we all originally had brown eyes. But about 10,000 years ago, someone who lived near the Black Sea developed a genetic mutation that turned brown eyes blue. While the reason blue eyes have persisted remains a bit of a mystery, one theory is that they act as a sort of paternity test. "There is strong evolutionary pressure for a man not to invest his paternal resources in another man's child," says the lead author of a study on the development of our baby blues. Because it is virtually impossible for two blue-eyed mates to create a brown-eyed baby. Therefore, this evolution has taken place, in the blue-eyed male ancestors, who very likely may have sought out blue-eyed mates as a way of ensuring fidelity. This would partially explain why, in a recent study, blue-eyed men rated blue-eyed women as more attractive, compared to brown-eyed women. Whereas females and brown-eyed men expressed no preference. This is a perfect example of how our bodies have evolved.

You can observe examples of evolution as it happens

If you are observant, and watchful, you can carefully witness the miracles of evolution as it is taking place. Some may not be good examples, as it has been discovered that the human species is growing older at a younger age. Signs of grey hair is found on individuals as young as nineteen. And senior citizens as old as eighty years of age, in body-building contests. In the past, our human bodies were known to live for hundreds of years before dying. Now, to live at the age of one hundred is considered an anomaly. But even still, you can see how we have changed as a species altogether.

The Importance of Discipline

Evolutionary biologists have long concentrated on the role of new mutations in generating new traits. But once a new mutation has arisen, it must spread through a population. Every person carries two copies of each gene, but the copies can vary slightly within and between individuals. Mutations in one copy might increase height; those in another copy, or allele, might decrease it. If changing conditions favor, say, tallness, then tall people will have more offspring, and more copies of variants that code for tallness will circulate in the population.

Human mutation has long been a subject of study that have held fascination for biologists, and scientists over the world. We as a species are constantly evolving to adapt to our environment. Our bodies have adjusted to climatize itself to our ever-changing world.

However, evolution is not simply about mutation. There are signs that we are evolving as people in culture and connections. The way we interact with each other, and how we socialize. In the past, there were many restrictions on what we can do, and how we choose to display our love for one another. Even the ability to have children.

History has come a long way in developing us as a people. Even if for many individuals they may not agree with the way our species has grown as a whole.

Researchers have gone over surveys and documentation where it is discovered that many people prefer the days of old. Where women were not as independent as freely outspoken. And men were the primary bread winners, that the laws were favored to be based around.

It is found that in our evolution of our culture, we have had to make many compromises that not everyone is in agreement with. But with evolution comes change. Whether you are ready for it or not. And our world is constantly changing. It is depiction of growth that is constantly being developed and adjusted. But there has been evidence as well as a decline, in an otherwise technology filled environment. Setbacks that can threaten the advance of our thriving evolution.

There are signs that you can take note of that will give you evidence of this. While our world is still constantly evolving, it is still very vulnerable to being thrown back into the stone ages, where we are completely dependent upon nothing but our own wits.

It has been discussed and debated time and again, how the evolution of our planet and people are severely subjected to technologies' power. The power and control of electronics, and social media. What would happen to us all if there were no more internet? If there were no electronics, and no computers? How would we as a culture be able to live in a world of the past, that we have evolved so far from?

I believe you can answer that question for yourself. It would be very difficult to do so. In our world today, our planet revolves around the use of technology. Computers, phones, electronics, our homes, cars, even how we get our food. It is all tied into technology. If for some reason, a plug was pulled, and our world became dark, what would we all do? Our evolution is a wonderful thing. However, it is based solely on the thriving success of technologies' power. Our culture has developed a dangerous dependency on something that we cannot control. We have trained ourselves to completely rely on the working functions of our cell phones, and computers in order to communicate. We no longer exercise our minds in finding other ways to speak to someone. It is so easy to rely on something that is readily at your fingertips. The problem is, no one ever considers the probability of having that easy access suddenly removed.

Ask yourself, if there were no computers, no internet, no electricity and no cell phones. Would we still be an evolved people? Are we basing our evolution on the success of technology? Or do we truly understand that evolution is based around the ability to comprehend and adapt, to communicate on our own without assistance? If technology was absent, would our world still function smoothly? Would we be able to adapt, or would we suddenly be thrown back into the stone ages, and resort to acting like cave men and women once again?

Our evolution must not be based solely on the reliance of technology and what it can do for us. Yes, we as a people have evolved with the knowledge that gave us the ability to create these things. Which is great. However, the knowledge is not in the technology. It is within us, as a human species. Therefore, we should be able to adapt to any environment, whether with the assistant of this technology or not.

Evolution is the growth of our humanity. Our minds developing into a stronger state of being. With the knowledge we have obtained over the years, our culture should not be dependent upon technology to keep us going. It is an asset, but should not be used as a crutch. We should regular as a people, take time away from these things such as cell phones, computers and electronics. Not simply because they can become addictive if used over a prolonged amount of time. But also because of the importance of have self-dependency, and self-discipline.

It is never wise to completely rely on any device or system to keep your world functioning and moving smoothly. The pure meaning of evolution is the purpose of being more. Having the knowledge of self to enable you to have and accomplish the things you desire. All with your own self-reliance and ingenuity. To truly evolve within yourself, you must become what you were created to be. A species that has the abilities to adapt to anything.

Chapter 14 – Why black lives matter

The first man was black. Everything originated from black. You must go through the darkness in order to get to the light. Black evokes strength and dominance. Strong emotions. However too much black can be overwhelming, fearsome and dangerous to the narrow minded and normal eye.

Black is beautiful, authoritative, powerful. It represents power, sophistication, elegance, formality, mystery and the unknown. This is everything it exudes.

Talented, gifted and intelligent, is what they should have been telling us. Instead they try to keep their race empowered. That's been the other race's biggest fears. The black man.

There's two types of women in this world. The ones that desire to be with a black man, and the ones that already are, with some of them staying away from that notion. Why? Some of us has fallen into the statistic America had planned for us. To be honest, most of us do not have our act together. Some of us have ten kids with five plus different baby mothers. Some are still in the street, or in jail. We have to be better. Our situations are tougher, but let's use that as motivation, and get and create an outlet.

There are plenty of ways to be fortunate besides being a rapper or a black ball player. One of the things you don't see in the news is how over 300,000 blacks (males and females) have enrolled in college. Don't be a product of your environment. We are not lucky, we make our own luck. There are plenty of people who are taken at face value.

I am a man that is required to constantly transform to meet expectations. Then transform once again to exceed expectations. My accomplishments are not one thing, because I am not one thing. I used all my experiences to my advantage, and now I dominate. Before I say this next sentence, I have police officers and lawyers I know whom are in the field and are personal friends, but I will say this. I believe police officers are programmed to target blacks and Hispanics. It's like a quota they must meet.

As sad as it is to say and write this, look at it this way. When a lion hunts for the pride, it or they search for a big buffalo rather than a little rabbit. Why? Because a buffalo can feed an entire pride and more.

When I have children one day, they will learn how to speak and act accordingly, with authority. Because of the privileges they lack. This is a book I would love my future children to look at and read.

Blacks are like a high commodity. Especially the black man. There are plenty of things that are going on in this world that has to stop, but continues to get pushed under the rug. We are urged to remember things in this world, like the holocaust, 9/11 but not the civil rights movement. Not slavery, not the Egyptians. Not the fact that the lighter skinned slaves were in the house, and the darker skinned slaves were outside. They were darker because of the sun. And the mixed babies by the slave owners who raped the black women, wanted their children inside. While white women hid their affairs with the black slave men, because they saw strength, stamina, muscle and aggression.

Some white women would force the slaves to have sex with them. Some would cry rape. In this world what I learned is, if you are fair skinned or white, you will always benefit from white supremacy.

I understand celebrities do not speak on it. Others do not speak on it, because of endorsements, brands, fans they would lose. Myself, I do not care. See when my people read this, they will cheer me on. Why? Because I say things they can't. I say things they are afraid to articulate. So when they realize there's a guy like myself around, it excites them. Because I make them desire to be what they want to be. What they want to say and do.

The Importance of Discipline

Before I had an outlet to speak or write, I used to hope celebrities read what I wrote, because they have the power to move people.

They are public figures, and people look up to them regardless of whether they want to be role models or not. And when they started speaking out, I knew I was making some noise.

Tupac Shakur once said: "I'm not saying I'm gonna change the world. But I guarantee that I will spark the brain that will change the world."

There is no NFL, NBA, boxing or track and field without black athletes. Their entire multi-billion dollar sports economy would collapse without participation of the black athletes. So I say, dear black people, it is ok to speak to each other when we walk pass each other. Because as a black man, I could never be good unless my brother is good too. How many of our ancestors died, or were seriously injured fighting hate with love? Being black is a blessing.

Certain things and people must be held accountable.

Haiti was the first black nation to become independent in 1804. America loves everything about us, but us. Why does America hate us? Where would America be without us? OnceYouGoBlack. Kings. Descendants. Chocolate. The original kings. Original DOMINANCE. Genetically inclined to reign supreme. Blacks built every pyramid you heard of, but the only thing they are allowed to know about themselves is slavery, and the civil rights movement. After all, Egyptians were not white. Firstly, Egypt is in Africa. The world's greatest fear is when the Black men unite. There were no reading or writing, and they created a savage of men. They killed any slave that could read, however, they gifted them with the Bible. In 1 Timothy 6:1, " let as many bondservants as are under the yoke count their own masters worthy of all honor, so that the name of God and his doctrine may not be blasphemed." In other words, all whom are under the yoke of slavery should consider their masters full of respect, so that God's name and our teaching may not be slandered.

The Bible was written, then re written, and re written again. Knowledge is a powerful weapon. Arm yourself with it. I'm blessed today, that you witness the power in my pen. First Kings, then into slaves, activists, black panthers into the penitentiary looking like a plantation again. One day, you will witness an immaculate win. Do I believe half of them in there are innocent? Absolutely. I don't know if black boys are magic, but I'm definitely magic. I say it, I do it. I speak it into existence. For me, the little things make a huge difference in life. I don't crave it, or wish. I deserve it, and I demand it. Believe that you deserve it, and the universe will serve it.

The Importance of Discipline

Where would America be without blacks? African blacks, Caribbean blacks, Hispanic blacks. American blacks. Indians. Etc. Absolutely nowhere. So why aren't blacks given more credit? America is so fascinated with black erotica. They love our big brains, our melanin skin, our athleticism, our music, voice, sports, muscular bodies, our creativity, our inventions. Our stamina. Our endurance. Our jokes. Our comedy. Our powerful seed. Let's be frank, we are what all the fuss is about in America. They don't care about all the other races, it's usually, "what are the blacks up to? What's the newest thing or idea they have going on? What else can we steal and claim as our own? Eighty five percent of the news is some type of crime of a black or Hispanic committed. This is the subjection of white supremacy. Everything else in the news is dirt that gets pushed under the rug. Now I'm going to get really personal now.

In the 1800's, and even earlier, they had the black women that were inside slaves breast feed the white babies, to keep them healthy and strong. As they realized how strong, and Dominant the black genes were. Some celebrities would go to Africa and adopt black babies. Back to genetics.....we have the most Dominant genes in the world. They want their lips full. Our Queens (Latinas, blacks, Europeans, etc) have that. They want their butts big, our Queens have that. Take myself for example, I only workout three times a week to look like this, meanwhile someone else would need to work six days to look half as good. And I don't take any performance enhancing drugs either. Now I'm going to get real personal once again.

We teach most of you slang. We teach you style. Essence. We teach you how to color coordinate with your clothes. We teach you confidence. Dominance. Aggression. How we walk. We make others insecure when we are in the building. We show love to everyone, even though we do not need to. (Black people can never be racist, we were the ones that were oppressed). We train you how to be cool. We teach you how to speak to the ladies, how to get with the ladies, and how to keep the ladies. We are the ones that turn them into freaks. Who displays more affection to the more curvier women? We've given women confidence to love their curves and big butts. The music and the culture women gravitate to.

For example, if you're at a party or club, and reggae or hip hop comes on. Women will seek out more black men, assuming we know how to vibe with those tunes better than any other race. Women love chocolate. They become addicted to it. Out of all the races, black men have the highest level of testosterone. Most women gravitate subconsciously towards the stronger genes. And black men exude strong genes. That energy, that's a change in the air, when we step into the building.

There were times, white bouncers would not allow myself or a friend of mine into a venue, because we were dressed too professionally, whether we had on designer or suits. And that's only because, they didn't want us attracting all the attention. We had money as well, why not us? We exude a sexual energy that women pick up on. An energy that women love, and inspires their comfort right away. Protection, strength, love, Dominance. Royalty is in our DNA. Loyalty is in our DNA. Knowledge of self is imperative. I mean, what if the lion did not know it was an apex predator? Black men, three things you need to understand about yourselves. One, your seed is life to all humanity, two, confidence, courage, power and strength are your allies. Three, you are King.

Why are most young black men from demographics of low income? They make it hard for blacks to get high quality loans. Therefore, we are placed in low income homes. Low income neighborhoods. Now, these men become a product of their environment. On the streets selling weight? You can take this question and play around with it a lot. If people knew how hard it was out here in these streets, well take this question this way. Our brothers and sisters go to school to get all these degrees, and just because of the color of his skin will not get hired, leading him to take lower paying jobs or going into a job not related into the field he or she studied for.

Then our brothers (mostly men locked up, not women) are getting locked up because of the color of their skin, so now with a criminal record who is going to hire our brothers?? Which leads our brothers into desperation. So you can twist this question a bunch of ways. Girls like the drug dealers because their willing to spend and throw it away vs a brother working and saving. These girls love the money and easy life with these brothers.

The women, have a different mindset when it comes to this. Queens uplift Kings and Kings uplift Queens. A Queen will always assist a King, and make sure he's always on top of his game. Why do black lives matter? How boring would it be without us?

What is a spirit?

A spirit is a form of energy. Energy is a form of frequency that carries a ritual. Energy carries information; this makes your blood spiritual. Your blood is your spirit, and your spirit is your blood. Frequencies of your blood is very high because it distributes signals/information through your body to your biochemical structure, and your biochemical structure downloads these signals/information. Your spirit is the bridge to your soul. This is why black people have to stop giving out blood. Even when your blood (spirit) leaves your body, it is still connected to you.

The blood is the assistant to your melanin. Melanin is also your antenna for the messages that are being displayed, or picked up by the blood. Your blood has an amount of slides, which bases counts on the nucleus. This is how doctors can tell how long you're going to live, due to the slides in your blood. And the nucleus connects you to the dream world. Keep your blood, beautiful black gods and goddesses.

Do black people have super power genes?

Yes, black people do. Melatonin (Melanin) is a high power spiritual living molecule. Melanin is also associated with your skin, causing it to be brown/black. But just because you are black, does not mean you have a high percentage of melanin. Remember that your percentage of melanin can be killed by certain foods. Frequencies that come from certain music, sounds, chemicals, too much TV, lack of sunlight, and most of all (not knowing the truth about your history) Melanin contains memories of your ancestors; so the more melanin you have, the more information and knowledge you can pull in through yourself without even putting your head in a book. Every living thing has to have melanin. White people have it also, but they have the lowest percentage of melanin than any race on earth.

Reasons Behind Americans Seeing Black People as a Threat

In recent events, there have been shootings of black men by white police officers that have highlighted a deep, uncomfortable truth about many Americans: They fear black men.

This has been a proven fact that the media showcases time and again. The fear of black men has been heightened to an extensive degree. Portraying them as violent and angry people that do not take care of their children or families. And are gangsters that run drug trafficking rings. There is research by Holbrooks that speak about this in depth.

He has a theory about why these American tragedies seem to keep repeating.

Holbrooks research became part of the national conversation last summer when he published a study in the journal Evolution and Human Behavior showing that people imagine blacks and Hispanics to be larger than they really are. Holbrook created stories about white and black men, making sure that the characters had stereotypical names for their race (Wyatt, Connor, or Garrett for white men; Jamal, DeShawn, or Darnell for black men). He then asked participants to imagine their characters. Were they aggressive? Were they respectable? Would you be afraid of them?

"If you look at the data, [whites and blacks] are about the same height and weight," Holbrook tells Inverse, pointing to figures that suggest the average American black man is just over five feet, nine inches tall and weighs roughly 196 pounds. The average American white man? Just over five feet, nine inches tall and roughly 196 pounds. No difference.

As he discovers, this is very common. Blacks and whites have been the same size for a long time. What is interesting, he notes, is how that size is perceived in light of preconceptions about "prestige."

This is why many individuals have relied on the size and appearance of the black man, to be construed as dominating, and threatening. The larger the man, the more violent he must be.

The media depiction of the black man is largely in part as to why the misconception has remained enforced when it comes to black people. Why people of other races, especially Caucasians, tend to become nervous and fearful when black people enter a store. Additional research shows more in detail the origins of this.

Neuberg says conscious organisms tend to believe in two overlapping worlds: a "desperate" one, where the environment is harsh and unpredictable, and predators abound, and a "hopeful" one, where an organism is predictably comfortable. He indicates that humans sort people by which world they come from. People from the less predictable world are treated as dangerous aliens, even as genuinely dangerous people from the comfortable world (like bank owners and white-collar working individuals) are perceived to be of higher standing. Blackness is the catalyst for this sort of thinking, but reactions become unpredictable because of a disconcerting otherness that is not purely a product of racial difference.

Do you comprehend the outlook here? It is strictly a very narrow view of how the world, particularly Americans, see black people as a whole. They believe they are lower class individuals that deserve to be treated as such. Now, not everyone feels this way. This is true. However, due to the mass media image of what the public has received, this is what is perceived and continued to believe.

Even when prominent black men and women, (not necessarily celebrities) make their presence known, it still comes as such a surprise to the general public. And it is expressed to the highest. You will hear things like: Wow! The first black man to own a bank in, etc. Or the first black woman to win an Olympic medal in, etc. Even the black communities celebrate, because of the huge accomplishment of being able to break through the vicious cycle of the image of the: No good black man or woman.

In a diverse country like the United States, race complicates everyone's story. Neuberg says that in general, young men tend to have stereotypes of being more criminal, more impulsive, and more dangerous. The narratives we imagine for black men are particularly bleak. The problem, in other words, is both the reality born of historical prejudice and injustice, and the fantasy, born of a natural impulse and subconscious prejudice.

The only way to change this mode of thinking, is to not live within the expectations that this world has set for you. As a black man myself, (Haitian/Dominican) it is challenging no matter where I go, or what I do. I am constantly being watched and assessed. Therefore, I choose my actions wisely. As a black man in America, everything you do is analyzed. You can be as good as any other man, however that will never be good enough. You have to be better, perform better, reach higher than all others, in order to be recognized. And even then, many will not want to give you a chance at success.

This is the world we live in. Because of the image that has been built. Having said that, of course there are those just like anyone else that have made bad decisions. But an entire race of people should never be blamed for the actions of a few. But it will always be the case. Because that is the world we live in. We must take the time and educate ourselves to being more, therefore we will have more. Is it possible to change the world? Holbrook notes that immigrants in other countries face similar economic barriers and racial prejudice and suggests that this might be a deeply ingrained human response to the other. (It's a particularly distressing fact given that the vast majority of black Americans come from American families.) And while education can help ease tensions, it's important to confront the reality that the human brain reacts to stimuli in illogical, but scientifically comprehensible ways when under stress.   "These are deeply entrenched concepts in the mind," Holbrook says. "There's no simple educational moment that's going to flip these ideas."

So think for yourself. And become the exception. Not the rule.

Chapter 15 – Accountability

Why Is Accountability So Important?

Any manager worth their weight in salt will assign authority to match responsibility for tasks they assign to team members. To do less than this only sets the other person up for failure. But along with authority and responsibility comes accountability – the understanding by all that the person assigned the responsibility is accountable for meeting their commitments and producing results. All too often though, and I've seen it happen repeatedly in every one of the eight industries I've worked in, a task is assigned to someone and they commit to completing the task but then ....nothing happens!

How many of us have seen a commitment made by someone in a meeting without a target date being set for completion? Or a course of action being identified without it being assigned to any one person for ownership and ultimate accountability? My experience has been that, in these situations, the likelihood of the necessary follow up action being taken - as required or as promised - is remote. People are busy and if you aren't tracking commitments that other people make to you, they may not deem those commitments with as high a priority….and be only too happy to let them slide or possibly not complete them at all. I'm sure you've seen commitments being made haphazardly by someone who has no expectation that anyone will actually track what they have committed to.

In order for a project to move ahead successfully, each task or action must be assigned so that one person is given ownership of it, along with a target date for completion and the appropriate responsibility, authority, and accountability. This is the first step. After a task has been assigned (by a manager or a group), there must be some form of follow up to confirm that the work is actually being done. This is where I've seen countless repeated occurrences of issues being dropped – because they are forgotten or outright ignored.

It never ceases to amaze me how often a lack of accountability comes up in a business day. Quality output and the successful completion of any project depends on people living up to their commitments. That's the grease that makes a team work well together. When people fulfill their commitments, they are showing everyone else that they're reliable and that they respect the person they've made the commitment to.

Why am I writing about this? Because it rests at the heart of success on any project. If your team members are all conscientious and focused on getting their tasks done, a lack of accountability will be a minor issue. But occasionally I've seen people make shallow promises that they know no one else will actually keep track of. That would entail someone else having to manage them - which they know - we're all too busy to do.

People can rely on others to come through on their commitments - to be able to track, monitor and follow up with others on their commitments in a diplomatic and friendly way. This process really helps to reinforce accountability and it's done in a simple, non-confrontational way that prevents anything from slipping between the cracks.

Under the assumption that most of us are well meaning, the ball can get dropped simply because of the overwhelming volume of things we each have to do in a day. It is good for a manager to help foster success for everyone on their team, and they can do that by simply touching base with people regularly for updates on their deliverables and by proactively helping them stay on top of the tasks and target dates they've committed to.

It is up to everyone on a project team to meet their obligations, but it is also up to everyone on a team to hold each other accountable in a manner that fosters strong relationships within a supportive, congenial and productive working environment that everyone can be proud of. This combination can be dynamite!

Accountability means answering or accounting for your actions and results. It is something every leader wants more of from his or her team. Accountability is like rain— everyone knows they need it, but no one wants to get wet. It's easy to talk about how "they" need to be more accountable, but it can be uncomfortable when we apply it to ourselves. When is the last time you heard someone say, "I really need to be more accountable for my results?" It doesn't happen very often. Yet we get more accountability from our teams by being accountable to them. It's a two-way street.

Although almost every organization you know, struggles to some extent with accountability, retailers tend to do a better job of boosting accountability than most. A primary reason is the specificity of their performance metrics and expectations. The bottom line is that accountability means letting your actions rise above your excuses.

At its core, accountability is really about specificity— specific expectations, specific consequences, and specific language. Take a moment now to reflect on the performance of each team member. Think of the lowest-performing team member. By default, that person's level of performance sets the standard for acceptable performance on your team—it's the performance level that you as the leader allow. It's a very public and visible standard regardless of how much we might want to sweep it under the rug or turn a blind eye to it. Winning leaders realize that they owe it to their team to always raise that standard, and it can be done by getting specific. Ambiguity is the Achilles' heel of accountability, but specificity enables you to raise the standards of your team's performance.

Receiving Specific Consequences

There is always a consequence to your actions. In everything that you do. This was discussed in a previous segment of the book. You must be willing to receive these consequences to things that you have done, and take your due with honor and integrity. Not only will you feel better for having gotten it over with, it will display your level of maturity when you do so.

External performance is ultimately a reflection of internal commitment.

Performance is what you will always be judged on, when in the working place. And even in relationships. How people perceive you, and react to you, will be directly reflective around your interaction with them. You must hold yourself accountable for how you treat others. Because there will be consequences to whatever performance you choose to display. Keep in mind that this is something that should be ingrained in you from young. If it has not been, then you must train your mind to perform at a level that is not just acceptable, but exceptional.

Accountability in Christianity

As Christians, there is a completely different level of accountability that is held within their circles. These are individuals that hold themselves to a very high standard of performance, based on their beliefs and teachings from the holy bible. The reason I want to discuss this particular topic is to outline some very key facts that sets Christians apart from everyone else. And how it has also been abused in our culture, as a form of discipline to enforce order and structure. People that follow the Christian religion have as of late been viewed as righteous freaks. People who look down on others and view them as sinners if they do not follow their ways. However, on the flip side, other individuals tend to hold Christians accountable, even if they do not display this type of condemning behavior. Once people hear that someone is a Christian, they automatically believe you should act and conduct yourself in a certain type of manner. Therefore, it can be challenging for them on both sides.

Believing in God alone, automatically holds you to a standard of accountability you must adhere to. You cannot say you believe in him, then act and perform in a way that displays people whom do not believe. Being held accountable for your beliefs and behavior, are high standards in the Christian community. If you are not ready to follow the rules and structure that this life holds, then do not proclaim to be a part of it.

There are many different forms of accountabilities we will touch on in this book. I will outline a few of them, and breakdown each one in clarification, so that you can understand the differences between all of them.

Spiritual Accountability

Regardless of your religious background, you should have a sense of spiritual accountability. A connection with a higher power that centers you and helps you to become a better person. Some people utilize yoga, exercise and various forms of ways to channel their spiritual self and retain peace in their life and environment.

This is something that is used in personal growth and development as well. It can help you to focus on your goals and obtain perspective on your achievements. You should always have a spiritual accountability that keeps you grounded. One of the reasons for this, is that it fuels your day. Stopping to pray in the morning before leaving out. Or ending the day in meditation, to alleviate all the stress of the day.

If you are a leader or in any form of team authoritative role, this is something that is paramount. Even if you choose not to use prayer, helping your team in a spiritual foundation can help take them further in all they want to accomplish. Having a firm foundation that your team can fall back on, will be beneficial to everyone in the long run.

Personal Accountability

With personal accountability, you have a more in-depth perspective on bringing yourself to a certain standard. This is the type of accountability in which you cannot escape, as your own conscious, and guilt will come into play here. Holding yourself accountable goes a long way in making you into a better person. If you can stick to your own self-disciplined guidelines, that you have made for yourself. And not allow anything to make you deviate from it. How can you make yourself more accountable? Follow your own rules that you have set in place for yourself. This can be challenging; however, you know what your own sense of self-preservation stands for. Your conscious is there to remind you when you are aware that what you're doing is wrong. Regardless of this, there are many that ignore their conscious and go against their better judgement. Again, this goes back to what we discussed regarding consequences and receiving them. You have to hold yourself accountable for what you do, more than anything else. Especially, if there are others that look up to you, and rely on you.

In this sense, you understand why it is crucial for you to hold yourself to a certain standard. Your actions not only reflect you, but they can directly impact those around you.

Having a Ministry Accountability

Ministry accountability speaks to the specific measures of accountability that you want to set for your team or organization, related to weekly ministry engagement. This should be a set of standards that uphold a level of excellence in your ministry. This means setting clear expectations for things like being on time, how to handle a discipline issue, contacting your students, employees, etc.

In this area of accountability, you must always set an example. Very similar to personal accountability, as a leader or in charge of an organization, or even the head of a family o group. Being the leader, you must set this standard, and be consistent that it is followed. Hold your people accountable, and they will adhere to the rules you have arranged in place.

Instilling Growth Accountability

Growth accountability is a more general area, but this is simply an area of accountability that sets expectations for all involved to always be seeking to be better this year than they were last year in all that they are doing. This leans heavily on you to offer training and resources to aid this process, but without a commitment to this from your leaders, you can't expect them to attend your training sessions in the first place.

Having Accountability vs responsibility.

Many people do not understand the difference between the two. In this section, I will outline the significance and how it affects you. First you must comprehend what it means and how we use it in our daily lives.

Having accountability is when you hold yourself to a certain standard. You have a rule that you live by, and you are left with the choice to follow it, or go against what you believe. Responsibility is something else. You are obligated to fulfill whatever you have been tasked with. There are no exceptions to this rule. If you break a responsibility, there are often severe consequences, possibly even jail time. Who does this affect? Everyone. You need to understand that being responsible means you are obligated, and must hold up your part to do what you have been given to do. This can be something like following the law, the rules of the workplace, etc. Responsibility can hold far more weight than accountability.

Why should you understand and know the difference between the two?

Because there will be many cooks in your kitchen.

People will forget who said what.

People will forget what they agreed to.

People will over promise and under deliver.

People will rearrange deadlines on you.

They will say that they were only responsible for one thing, not all the things you agreed they'd be responsible for.

People will always challenge your rules.

Another common misconception is that we can all be held accountable for the things we do on a project. All of us. The entire team. That we're all responsible and 'in this together for the common good'. This is common in small - medium creative agencies.

If you look up the definition of 'communism' you will find that the common thread through it is as follows:

A theory or system of social organization in which all property is owned by the community and each person contributes and receives according to their ability and needs. Communism isn't that successful for a reason.

When communications/design/strategy projects lack the fundamental clarity of assigning accountability and responsibility. They're doomed.

If you, as a Creative Leader don't know the difference, you're contributing to that doom. You must be ready to handle these many aspects that can create havoc on your patience and time. People don't often enjoy following rules. However, they will be obligated as their responsibility to obey them, if they do not want to receive the ensuing consequences that comes with insubordination.

ACCOUNTABILITY in LIFE

Accountability is the precipice in life. Different from responsibility, it keeps you in line with yourself, and the comprehension of right versus wrong. Harvard Business Review wrote that one out of every two managers are terrible at accountability. That means that it's pretty much a guarantee that you'll know someone or are currently working for someone who has no idea what leadership actually means. There is a distinct separation between accountability and responsibility.

Many leaders have no clue how to hold themselves accountable. They are stricken with the belief that in time everyone will simply fall in line. This is far from the truth. To be accountable means you need to demonstrate extreme ownership over a situation and within your team. Success of failure — that success or failure is yours if you're accountable.

Accountability is about owning a commitment you've made and delivering on it. Accountability is also being completely responsible for all the responsibilities — all the commitments. It means carefully structuring a plan that everyone must follow and then seeing that plan through. Harvard Business Review states it well: "It's complete responsibility to an outcome, not just a set of tasks. It's taking initiative with thoughtful, strategic follow-through."

Accountability cannot be shared. Only one person can be held accountable.

To make it clearer for example, when completing a project, the project owner is accountable for that project's success. They drive the project, they build and drive the team. They manage expectations with clients and ensure that the project delivers the agreed outcome. If the project succeeds, they get a pat on the back. If it doesn't, you can be sure there'll be a meeting held with them asking them why.

In a more concise way of breaking it down this is what you need to do:

In any situation, set clear expectations. Be crystal clear and make sure you both understand one another.

Clarify capabilities. Can they complete the project? Do they have all the resources?

Clarify how success will be measured. Define what 'done' looks like.

Give very clear feedback. Don't beat around the bush. Be direct. Be honest.

Set clear consequences.

UNDERSTANDING RESPONSIBILITY

Responsibility can be shared. You must understand why Accountability cannot.

In this instance, you need to comprehend why it is essential that the two are clearly defined. When the project owner meets with the team, and the team decides who will handle the strategy, the design, the art direction and the research — each individual in team essentially takes responsibility for those tasks.

There have been a few cases, in which these tasks might turn into mini-projects within a project. If you're doing one of them, you're responsible. If you're doing the art direction, you're responsible for the art direction. If you're doing the strategy, you're responsible for the strategy.

If there is confusion as to who is responsible. It's your job to ask and it's the project owner's job to make it clear to you.

You need to learn to work together.

Always keep in mind:

Only one person should be accountable.

Many people can be responsible.

It's OK to hold people accountable.

Responsibility can be shared, accountability cannot.

If everyone is responsible for one thing, no one is responsible for that thing.

Always inform your people of the things they're accountable and responsible for.

This will always be a heavy burden on you because of your status as the leader. You must lead by example, and continue to set the rules everyone must adhere to. As long as you hold yourself accountable for your actions, the people around you will hold themselves responsible for the rules you set in place.

About the Author

Born and raised in New York, E.L Discipline is educating the masses on the true form of spiritual connections. With his second book, The Importance of Discipline, he aims to impart his knowledge of the inner workings of leadership and development. How to adapt to any environment around you, and becoming more in control of the dynamics of your future.

As a fitness trainer, he mentors and teaches about endurance not only in the body, but the mind as well. His will to dominate has pushed him to master a variety of enterprises. His books are taking the world by storm, and his education speaks volumes. His goal is clear, as he has one main purpose in mind: To change the world, one reader at a time.

www.ingramcontent.com/pod-product-compliance
Lightning Source LLC
Chambersburg PA
CBHW021227090426
42740CB00006B/424